ADIRONDACK STORIES
Historical Sketches

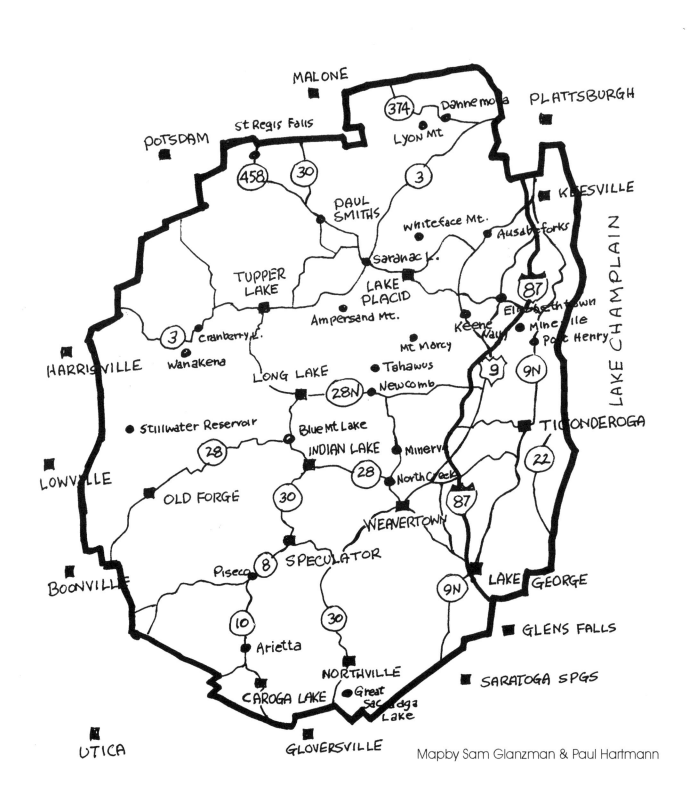

MALONE

PLATTSBURGH

374   Dannemora

POTSDAM   St Regis Falls

LYON Mt

458   30   3   KEESVILLE

PAUL SMITHS

whiteface Mt.   Ausdbeforks

TUPPER LAKE   Saranac L.

LAKE PLACID   87

3   Cranberry L.   Ampersand Mt.   Elizasethtown

HARRISVILLE   Wanakena   Keene Vall   Mineville

Mt Marcy   Port Henry

Long Lake   Tahawus   9   9N

28N   Newcomb

Stillwater Reservoir   Blue Mt Lake

LOWVILLE   INDIAN LAKE   Minerv   TICONDEROGA

28   28   North Creek   22

OLD FORGE   30   WEAVERTOWN   87

Piseco   8   SPECULATOR

BOONVILLE   9N   LAKE GEORGE

10   GLENS FALLS

Arietta   30   SARATOGA SPGS

NORTHVILLE

CAROGA LAKE   Great Sacradga Lake

UTICA   GLOVERSVILLE   Map by Sam Glanzman & Paul Hartmann

LAKE CHAMPLAIN

ADIRONDACK STORIES

Historical Sketches

Marty Podskoch, writer

Sam Glanzman, illustrator

David Hayden, editor

Podskoch PRESS

East Hampton, CT
2017

Adirondack Stories, Historical Sketches

First Edition 2007
Second Printing 2017

Published by
Podskoch Press, Ltd.
43 O'Neill Lane
East Hampton, CT 06424

podskoch@comcast.net
http://www.adirondackstories.com

ISBN 978-0-9971019-1-1

Manufactured in the United States of America

6 5 4 3 2 1
Cover illustration by Sam Glanzman
Design by Tim Parsons, Sandy Hildreth & Janet Atkins Hinterland Design
Map by Sam Glanzman & Paul Hartmann

CONTENTS

SPORTS

ENTERTAINMENT

MYSTERIES & MONSTERS

CRIME

DISASTERS

MISCELLANEOUS

New York State's Adirondack region has one of the largest bodies of literature recorded for any geographic location in our country. The forested mountains played a major role in the formation of our nation. The waters of the Adirondacks have an endless history from the early transportation routes to the growth of permanent settlements. Second homes and camps sprang up on the lakes for those who came to seek the many benefits of The North Country. Recreational opportunities have played a role in Adirondack history. And the health-giving features of the "Great North Woods" brought the rich and famous along with citizens of all stations to seek the healing powers found in the pure air and curing climate of the Adirondacks.

Adirondack pictures bring the past alive. Old photographs of loggers, tannery workers, river drivers, hunters, anglers, guides, guideboats, steamers, trains, log buildings, and other aspects of Adirondack life inspired Sam Glanzman's sketches of today, in the tradition of Verplanck Colvin, who drew dramatic and accurate illustrations of his early surveying expeditions. One famous 19th c. sketch can be found in *Appleton's Journal* of September 21, 1872. It is titled "Our Artist in the Adirondacks" and includes some fifteen sketches of life in the mountains. Marty Podskoch's stories with Sam's drawings, continue the long tradition of Adirondack sketching.

The 6,000,000-acre Adirondack Park of public and private lands has been home to an endless line of human players. Adirondack guides, railroad barons, great-camp owners, hotel keepers, artists, writers, surveyors, scientists, explorers, hermits, settlers and visitors, are among those whose stories appear in the written and illustrated record. Meeting them once more in these pages is a true delight. Marty Podskoch and Sam Glanzman have made a major contribution to the body of Adirondack literature by unearthing a wealth of unique Adirondack stories and illustrating them for our understanding.

Don Williams is the author of five books on the Adirondacks and a licensed Adirondack guide.

PREFACE

I had just finished my second book on the fire towers of New York, when my friend Sam Glanzman, an illustrator with over 50 years of experience in the comic book industry, called me in March 2004 and said, "I'm 80 years old and I need a project. Do you have any ideas?" At that time I had a lot of research for my book on the northern Adirondack fire towers and I suggested that we work together using both of our skills creating historical sketches, using words reinforced by pictures. Working with the format of pictures and words reminded me of my younger days when I enjoyed the visual aspect of comics. Do you remember reading *Classic Comic* books as a kid? I loved them and then I found out that Sam had drawn many of them.

It was my job to choose a topic, read as much material as I could on the subject, and then, the hardest job of all, condense it into about 150 words, which was the limit Sam could letter into the format of his illustrations. Luckily I had David Hayden, my editor, to keep me on the straight and narrow. It was awfully easy for me to go beyond the limit with all the information I had, but he was able to use a word or two, where I would use many more.

When I sent Sam the edited copy I included a variety of pictures for him to mull over. When he had something to show me, we'd meet at Morey's diner in Oneonta and he'd hand me the finished work. I was always amazed at his images and layouts. I couldn't believe my good fortune to be working with the illustrator of *Outdoor Life's* monthly article (1960-68), "It Happened to Me."

After I had some 8 1/2 X 11 examples, I went to newspapers in and around the Adirondacks. The editors and publishers were impressed and by the end of June 2004, our "Adirondack Stories" column was in six newspapers. The next two years some newspapers dropped out and were replaced by others. Presently there are six papers printing the articles on either a weekly or monthly basis.

Linda and Sarah Cohen of the Old Forge Hardware suggested that we make posters of our stories for people to hang in their camp. So we made some and started selling them to stores. When we got reorders we realized that people appreciated our vignettes and the illustrations, so I decided to take the next step, and combine them all into a book. I had been a reading teacher for most of my life and books were my teaching tool. I imagined that these brief stories would bring readers to want to know more about these unusual topics: personalities such as French Louie, Nick Stoner, and Paul Smith; bizarre events such as the sighting of Big Foot, the Great Windfall of 1845 and the unsolved mystery of Champ, the sea creature of Lake Champlain; the dangerous occupations of logging and mining; the magnificent architecture of the great camps of Sagamore, Nehasane, Santanoni, and Litchfield; the French & Indian and Revolutionary war battles that were fought in the Adirondacks; the famous artists, Georgia O'Keeffe, Frederic Remington, and Winslow Homer; and writers Ralph Waldo Emerson, and John Burroughs who were inspired by the beauty of the mountains and lakes.

Sam and I really enjoyed creating these sketches of Adirondack history and will continue our weekly newspaper column with more Adirondack Stories.

BEAVER

THE BEAVER, THE STATE MAMMAL OF NY, WAS SIGNIFICANT IN THE EXPLORATION AND COLONIZATION OF NEW YORK. THERE WERE ABOUT 1,000,000 BEAVER IN THE ADIRONDACKS IN THE 1600s WHEN THE SETTLERS ARRIVED. TRAPPING BEAVER WAS EXTENSIVE IN THE NEW WORLD AS EUROPEANS WANTED BEAVER PELT TO MAKE FELT HATS AND FUR TRIM ON CLOTHING. BY THE 1680s THE DUTCH HAD EXPORTED OVER 80,000 PELTS FROM FORT ORANGE (ALBANY). BY 1894 THERE WERE ONLY ABOUT 10 BEAVER LEFT IN THE ADIRONDACKS. THE NEXT YEAR THE STATE BANNED TRAPPING BEAVER. OVER THE NEXT 20 YEARS BEAVER WERE RESETTLED IN THE ADIRONDACKS FROM CANADA AND YELLOWSTONE PARK. BY 1921 THE POPULATION HAD GROWN TO ABOUT 20,000 AND TRAPPING WAS REOPENED IN 1924. TODAY THE DEC ESTIMATES THAT THERE ARE ABOUT 75,000 BEAVER IN THE ADIRONDACKS.

(1812)

(1815)

SOME BEAVER HATS

(1820)

(1825)

© 2006 MARTY PODSKOCH — SAM GLANZMAN

SABAEL BENEDICT

1745–1855

SABAEL BENEDICT, AN ABENAKI INDIAN, WAS ONE OF THE FIRST SETTLERS OF INDIAN LAKE IN CENTRAL HAMILTON COUNTY. LOCAL HISTORY SAYS HE WAS A PENOBSCOT INDIAN WHO LEFT MAINE AND JOINED THE CANADIAN ABENAKI TRIBE WHO FOUGHT WITH THE BRITISH. AT THE AGE OF 12 HE WITNESSED THE BATTLE OF QUEBEC IN 1759. DURING THE REVOLUTIONARY WAR HE LEFT CANADA AND SETTLED IN THE ADIRONDACKS' WILDERNESS. HE AND HIS WIFE AND FOUR CHILDREN LIVED IN A WIGWAM NEAR INDIAN LAKE. HIS WIFE IS BURIED NEAR SQUAW BROOK— WHICH IS WHY IT'S CALLED "SQUAW" AND HE MOVED HIS FAMILY ACROSS THE LAKE. ONE SON, ELIJAH, GUIDED PROFESSOR EMMONS'S GEOLOGICAL SURVEY AND DAVID HENDERSON WHOSE PARTY DISCOVERED IRON NEAR NEWCOMB. SABAEL LIVED TO ABOUT THE AGE OF 108. SOME SAY HE WAS MURDERED FOR HIS GOLD BY HIS SON. A HAMLET WAS NAMED AFTER HIM, AND INDIAN LAKE DERIVES ITS NAME BECAUSE OF HIS PRESENCE.

© 2005 MARTY PODSKOCH–SAM GLANZMAN

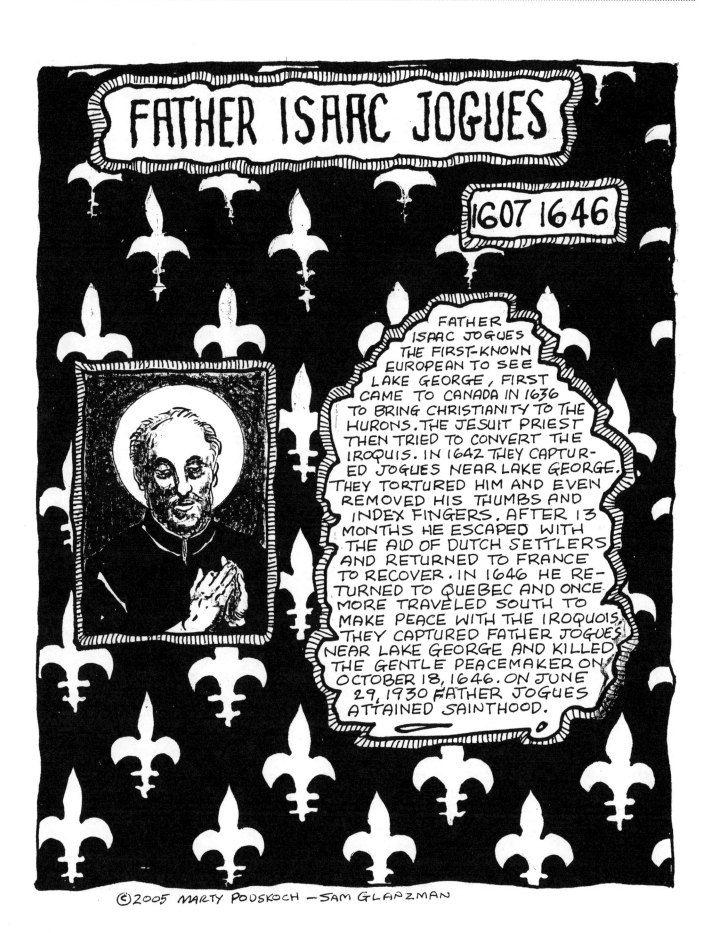

FATHER ISAAC JOGUES

1607 1646

FATHER ISAAC JOGUES THE FIRST-KNOWN EUROPEAN TO SEE LAKE GEORGE, FIRST CAME TO CANADA IN 1636 TO BRING CHRISTIANITY TO THE HURONS. THE JESUIT PRIEST THEN TRIED TO CONVERT THE IROQUIS. IN 1642 THEY CAPTURED JOGUES NEAR LAKE GEORGE. THEY TORTURED HIM AND EVEN REMOVED HIS THUMBS AND INDEX FINGERS. AFTER 13 MONTHS HE ESCAPED WITH THE AID OF DUTCH SETTLERS AND RETURNED TO FRANCE TO RECOVER. IN 1646 HE RETURNED TO QUEBEC AND ONCE MORE TRAVELED SOUTH TO MAKE PEACE WITH THE IROQUOIS. THEY CAPTURED FATHER JOGUES NEAR LAKE GEORGE AND KILLED THE GENTLE PEACEMAKER ON OCTOBER 18, 1646. ON JUNE 29, 1930 FATHER JOGUES ATTAINED SAINTHOOD.

© 2005 MARTY POUSKOCH — SAM GLARZMAN

EBENEZER EMMONS
1799   1863

EBENEZER EMMONS, A PHYSICIAN, NATURAL HISTORY PROFESSOR, AND GEOLOGIST LED A SURVEY TEAM TO EXPLORE NORTHERN NY--BEGINNING IN 1837. FOR FOUR YEARS HE TRAVELED THROUGH DENSE FORESTS AND COLLECTED SAMPLES AND TOOK MEASUREMENTS OF THE STATE'S GEOLOGY, BOTANY, ZOOLOGY, AND MINERALOGY. ON AUGUST 5, 1837 EMMONS MADE THE FIRST RECORDED ASCENT OF MOUNT MARCY AND NAMED IT AFTER THE GOVERNOR OF NEW YORK. IN 1838 EMMONS PROPOSED THE NAME "ADIRONDACKS" FOR THE REGION AFTER THE EARLY INDIAN TRIBE THAT HAD LIVED THERE. HIS REPORTS TO THE STATE LEGISLATURE STATED THE ADIRONDACK REGION WAS A LAND "UNRIVALED FOR ITS MAGIC AND ENCHANTMENT." HE PRAISED THE NATURAL RESOURCES & SCIENTIFIC WONDERS, WHICH ENTICED ENTREPRENEURS, AND IMMIGRANTS TO COME TO "THE GREAT NORTHERN WILDERNESS."

© 2005 MARTY PODSKOCH-SAM GLANZMAN

SIR WILLIAM JOHNSON

1715 ◆ 1774

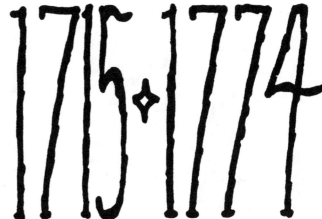

SIR WILLIAM JOHNSON COAT OF ARMS

DEO REGIQUE DEBEO

SIR WILLIAM JOHNSON COAT OF ARMS

SIR WILLIAM JOHNSON A POWERFUL BRITISH LEADER AND FOUNDER OF JOHNSTOWN, NY, HELPED KEEP THE IROQUOIS LOYAL TO ENGLAND. IN 1734 HE EMIGRATED FROM IRELAND AND SETTLED IN THE MOHAWK VALLEY WHERE HE TRADED WITH THE INDIANS AND EARLY SETTLERS. JOHNSON LIVED WITH THE MOHAWK, ADOPTED THEIR CUSTOMS AND DRESS, AND LEARNED THEIR LANGUAGE. HE WAS MADE A SACHEM (CHIEF) AND SAT AT THEIR COUNCIL MEETINGS. HE BUILT FORT JOHNSON AND IN 1763 HE BEGAN BUILDING JOHNSON HALL, THE NUCLEUS OF HIS ESTATE THAT GREW TO 400,000 ACRES. SIR WILLIAM HAD RELATIONS WITH MANY WHITE AND INDIAN WOMEN THAT RESULTED IN 20 CHILDREN. HE DID MARRY ONE INDIAN, MOLLY BRANT. IN 1755 WITH THE HELP OF THE MOHAWKS, JOHNSON DEFEATED THE FRENCH AT LAKE GEORGE. HE NAMED THE LAKE AFTER KING GEORGE II AND BUILT FORT WILLIAM HENRY. HE BECAME THE SUPERINTENDENT OF IROQUOIS AFFAIRS AND WAS MADE A BARONET. JOHNSON DIED IN 1774 WHILE LISTENING TO INDIAN GRIEVANCES.

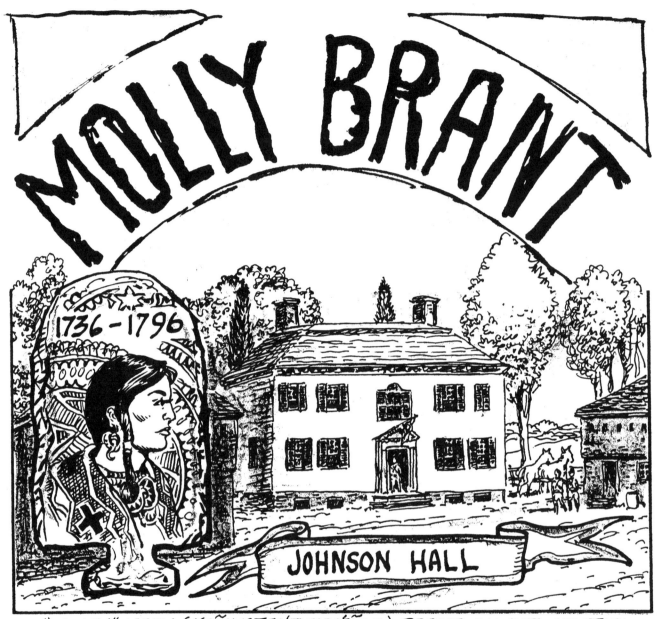

MOLLY BRANT

1736 - 1796

JOHNSON HALL

"MOLLY" MARY (KOÑWATSI'TSIAIÉÑNI) BRANT, AN INFLUENTIAL
MOHAWK INDIAN HELPED THE BRITISH AND AMERICAN LOYALISTS
DURING THE AMERICAN REVOLUTION. SHE WAS BORN IN CANAJOHARIE
OF INDIAN PARENTS BUT WHEN HER FATHER DIED HER MOTHER MAR-
RIED AN INDIAN NAMED, BRANT. HER BROTHER JOSEPH BRANT, BECAME
A FAMOUS MOHAWK CHIEF. SHE MARRIED WILLIAM JOHNSON (1715-
1774), A LAND BARON AND BRITISH SUPERINTENDENT OF INDIAN
AFFAIRS. THEY LIVED IN JOHNSON HALL IN PRESENT-DAY JOHNS-
TOWN, NY WHERE MOLLY RAISED THEIR SEVEN CHILDREN AND
ENTERTAINED IMPORTANT VISITORS. SHE VISITED MANY INDIAN
CHIEFS TO MAINTAIN THEIR LOYALTY TO THE BRITISH. WHEN WILLIAM
DIED IN 1774, SHE MOVED TO CANAJOHARIE BUT HAD TO FLEE TO
CANADA IN 1777 BECAUSE SHE WAS A LOYALIST.

© 2005 — MARTY PODSKOCH — SAM GLANZMAN

RAQUETTE LAKE'S NAME

RAQUETTE LAKE GOT IT'S NAME FROM, *raquette*, THE FRENCH WORD FOR SNOW-SHOES. JESUITS SAW INDIANS WEARING *raquettes*, WHILE HUNTING MOOSE NEAR THE LAKE. AROUND 1840 AMERICAN SETTLERS FOUND A LARGE PILE OF *raquettes* NEAR SOUTH INLET LEFT BY SIR JOHN JOHNSON, A BRITISH OFFICER, WHO AT THE OUTBREAK OF THE AMERICAN REVOLUTION IN 1777 FLED WITH A LOYALIST GROUP OF BRITISH SETTLERS AND INDIANS TO CANADA. LEAVING JOHNSTOWN IN THE DEAD OF WINTER, THE PARTY GOT TO THE LAKE AS THE SPRING THAW ARRIVED. THEY ABANDONED THEIR *raquettes* AND BUILT BIRCH-BARK CANOES AND CONTINUED ON TO THE ST. LAWRENCE RIVER AND TO SAFETY.

INDIAN *raquettes*

©2005 MARTY PODSKOCH - SAM GLANZMAN

17

FORT CARILLON

1755   1759

IN 1755 THE FRENCH BUILT FORT CARILLON WHERE THE WATERS OF LAKE GEORGE FLOW INTO LAKE CHAMPLAIN. IT CONTROLLED THE VITAL ROUTE BETWEEN CANADA AND NEW YORK CITY. IN JULY 1758 THE BRITISH SENT AN ARMY OF 16,000 UNDER LT. GEN. JAMES ABERCROMBY AND GEN HOWE TO ATTACK FORT CARILLON.

©MARTY PODSKUCH SAM GLANZMAN 2005

ON A HEIGHT OF LAND TO THE WEST OF FORT CARILLON, THE MARQUIS DE MONTCALM'S FRENCH TROOPS HAD BUILT A MASSIVE EARTH AND LOG-WORK FORTIFICATION PROTECTED BY A TREACHEROUS ABATTIS, A TANGLE OF BRUSH AND SHARPENED STAKES.

DURING THE DAY-LONG BATTLE WAVE AFTER WAVE OF AMERICAN PROVINCIAL AND BRITISH TROOPS INCLUDING THE 42ND HIGHLAND "BLACK WATCH" REGIMENT ASSAULTED THE FRENCH LINES, SUFFERED HUGE CASUALTIES AND WERE DEFEATED BY A FRENCH FORCE ¼ THEIR SIZE.

FRENCH·COAT·OF·ARMS

BRITISH·COAT·OF·ARMS

A YEAR LATER, BRITISH GENERAL LORD AMHERST CAPTURED FORT CARILLON AND RENAMED IT FORT TICONDEROGA.

FORT TICONDEROGA

THE CAPTURE OF FORT TICONDEROGA WAS THE FIRST AMERICAN VICTORY OF THE REVOLUTIONARY WAR. IN THE EARLY MORNING HOURS OF MAY 10, 1775, ETHAN ALLEN AND BENEDICT ARNOLD LED A GROUP OF 83 GREEN MOUNTAIN BOYS ACROSS LAKE CHAMPLAIN TO THE ENTRANCE TO FORT TICONDEROGA. AFTER A BRIEF ENCOUNTER WITH A LONE BRITISH SENTRY, THE REBELS FILED INTO THE FORT TO A SLEEPING BRITISH GARRISON OF 69 SOLDIERS, WOMEN AND CHILDREN. WHILE THE GREEN MOUNTAIN BOYS SECURED THE GARRISON, ETHAN ALLEN AND BENEDICT ARNOLD SUMMONED THE COMMANDING OFFICER DEMANDING THE SURRENDER OF THE FORT AND ALL ITS ARMAMENTS.

AFTER THE FORT WAS SURRENDERED, PLANS WERE MADE TO TRANSPORT TICONDEROGA'S CANNON TO THE ILL-EQUIPPED AMERICAN ARMY IN BOSTON. DURING THE WINTER OF 1775-1776 NEARLY 60 TONS OF ARTILLERY WERE TRANSPORTED TO BOSTON AND THESE CANNON WOULD ULTIMATELY FORCE THE BRITISH TO EVACUATE THE CITY IN THE SPRING OF 1776.

© 2004 MARTY PORSKOGL - SAM GLANZMAN

WHITEHALL

"BIRTHPLACE OF THE U.S. NAVY"

WHITEHALL, LOCATED AT THE SOUTHERN END OF LAKE CHAMPLAIN, IS CALLED THE BIRTHPLACE OF THE U.S. NAVY BECAUSE BENEDICT ARNOLD BUILT THE FIRST AMERICAN SHIPS THERE IN 1776. IT WAS ORIGINALLY CALLED SKENESBORO AFTER A FORMER BRITISH NAVAL CAPTAIN PHILIP SKENE FOUNDED A SETTLEMENT THERE IN 1759. SKENE SET UP A SAWMILL AND FOUNDRY AND BUILT SHIPS FOR TRADE ON LAKE CHAMPLAIN AND WITH THE WEST INDIES. PATRIOTS IN 1776 CONFISCATED SKENE'S MANOR AND MERCHANT SHIPS, WHICH WERE THEN ARMED FOR WAR AND RENAMED. IN 1776 ARNOLD BUILT MORE SHIPS IN SKENESBORO AND IN OCTOBER HE SAILED NORTH WITH THE 15 SHIPS OF THE US NAVY AND ATTACKED THE BRITISH AT VALCOUR ISLAND FORCING THE BRITISH TO RETREAT TO CANADA. THIS VICTORY GAVE OUR ARMY A YEAR TO GAIN STRENGTH AND DEFEAT THE BRITISH AT THE BATTLE OF SARATOGA IN OCTOBER 1777.

BENEDICT ARNOLD

FORT TICONDEROGA

GENERAL JOHN BURGOYNE 1722 1792

IN 1777, TWO YEARS AFTER THE AMERICANS SEIZED FORT TICONDEROGA FROM THE BRITISH, THE BRITISH ARMY RETURNED WITH A LARGE INVASION FORCE LED BY GENERAL JOHN BURGOYNE. AS THE BRITISH ARTILLERY WERE PREPARING TO BOMBARD THE FORT, THE AMERICAN ARMY ESCAPED UNDER COVER OF DARKNESS ON JULY 5. BURGOYNE LEFT A DETACHMENT OF ABOUT 200 MEN AT THE FORT AND WENT DOWN LAKE CHAMPLAIN TO-WARDS ALBANY BUT WAS DEFEATED AT SARATOGA. IN SEPTEMBER, COL. JOHN BROWN LED AN AMERICAN FOR-CE AGAINST FORT TICONDEROGA. DESPITE BEING OUT-NUMBERED 5-1 THE BRITISH WOULD'T SURRENDER. IN NOVEMBER THEY ABANDONED AND DESTROYED THE FORT.

© 2004 MARTY PODSKOCH — SAM GLANZMAN

FORT TICONDEROGA RUINS C. 1890

AFTER THE BRITISH DESTROYED FORT TICONDEROGA IN 1777, IT LAY IN RUINS FOR 132 YEARS. IN 1909 THE RESTORATION OF THE FORT BEGAN AND TODAY FORT TICONDEROGA IS A WORLD-CLASS MUSEUM WITH 100,000 TOURISTS VISITING EACH YEAR. THE FORT AND MUSEUM ARE OPEN TO THE PUBLIC FROM EARLY MAY TO LATE OCTOBER AND HOUSES ONE OF THE LARGEST 18TH CENTURY MILITARY ARTIFACT COLLECTIONS IN NORTH AMERICA. INTERPRETIVE PROGRAMS INCLUDE GUIDED TOURS OF THE FORT BY HISTORICALLY UNIFORMED SOLDIERS AND MUSKET FIRING DEMONSTRATIONS. CANNON FIRING, FIFE AND DRUM CORPS PERFORMANCES OCCUR DAILY DURING JULY AND AUGUST. FOR MORE INFORMATION VISIT THE MUSEUM'S WEBSITE WWW.FORT-TICONDEROGA.ORG.

FORT TICONDEROGA TODAY

THE CONTINENTAL ARMY EVENTUALLY ACQUIRED REGULATION UNIFORMS PURCHESED IN FRANCE.

© MARTY PODSKOCH — SAM GLANZMAN

1768 LAKE BONAPARTE 1844

© 2005
MARTY PODSKOCH
SAM GLANZMAN

LAKE BONAPARTE IN THE NORTHWEST ADIRONDACKS NEAR HARRISVILLE, WAS NAMED FOR JOSEPH BONAPARTE THE BROTHER OF THE FRENCH EMPEROR NAPOLEON AND THE FORMER KING OF SPAIN, WHO TRADED SOME CROWN JEWELS OF SPAIN AND MOVED TO AMERICA IN 1815. HE WANTED TO TAKE HIS BROTHER TO AMERICA BUT NAPOLEON HAD ASKED THE BRITISH FOR ASYLUM AFTER HIS DEFEAT AT WATERLOO, AND THEY EXILED HIM TO ELBA. JOSEPH BOUGHT 240,000 ACRES OF LAND IN JEFFERSON AND ST. LAWRENCE COUNTIES, WHERE HE INTENDED TO CREATE A "NEW FRANCE."

BONAPARTE BUILT A HUNTING LODGE ON THE HIGH ROCKY HILL ON THE EASTERN SHORE OF LAKE BONAPARTE. HE NAMED THE LAND "DIANA" AFTER THE ROMAN GODDESS OF THE HUNT. NEAR PRESENT-DAY NATURAL BRIDGE, HE BUILT A MANSION OVER THE NATURAL CAVERNS, WHICH LEGEND SAYS COULD BE USED AS ESCAPE ROUTES. JOSEPH BONAPARTE LEFT AMERICA IN 1839 AND WENT BACK TO ITALY.

SHAKER PLACE

BAKER'S PEEL

SHAKER PLACE WAS A SMALL RELIGIOUS COMMUNITY IN ARIETTA IN THE SOUTHERN ADIRONDACKS, WHICH BEGAN FARMING AND MAKING WOODEN FURNITURE IN 1810. THE SHAKERS WERE FOUNDED BY MOTHER ANN LEE IN 1772 IN ENGLAND WITH THE GOAL OF ATTAINING PERFECT HOLINESS. THEIR VIOLENT SHAKING AND SPEAKING IN TONGUES DISTINGUISHED THEM. IN 1774 LEE CAME TO AMERICA AND ESTABLISHED A SMALL FARMING COMMUNITY IN WATERVLIET THAT EMPHASIZED SIM—PLICITY, EQUALITY OF SEXES, CELIBACY, AND PEACE. NEW LEBANON, NY BE—CAME THE FIRST FORMAL SETTLEMENT IN THE 1780S. A GROUP OF ABOUT 12 SHAKERS LEFT NEW LEBANON AND STARTED A NEW SETTLEMENT IN ARI—ETTA ON PRESENT ROUTE 10 SOUTH OF PISECO LAKE. THE FOREST PROVIDED WOOD TO MAKE FURNITURE, HOUSEHOLD IMPLEMENTS LIKE SPOONS, PAILS, TUBS AND BAKER'S PEELS (FLAT WOODEN PADDLES TO REMOVE BREAD FROM AN OVEN.) THE SHAKERS ABANDONED THEIR 1,200 ACRES, MILLPOND, AND HOUSE IN 1820. IT IS SUGGESTED THEY LEFT BE—CAUSE MOOSE DESTROYED THEIR GAR—DENS.

©MARTY GLICKMAN 2007

DWELLING HOUSE 1800 "SHAKER PLACE"

VERPLANCK COLVIN

• THE MAN, HIS WORKS HIS DREAMS ARE LITTLE KNOWN TODAY •

1847 — 1920

WHILE WORKING AT HIS FATHER'S LAW OFFICE, COLVIN BECAME QUITE INTERESTED IN MAPPING AND SURVEYING. EXPLORING THE WILDS OF THE ADIRONDACKS HE SOON FELL IN LOVE WITH THEIR BEAUTY. •• SEEING THEM MINED, LOGGED, BURNED, AND RUTTED COLVIN BEGAN TO WRITE ARTICLES AND GAVE TALKS ABOUT THEM. HE WAS FIRST TO PROPOSE THEIR LEGAL PROTECTION. IN 1872 HE HELPED CONVINCE THE LEGISLATURE TO SURVEY AND MAP THE ADIRONDACKS. COLVIN SUPERVISED THE 28-YEAR PROJECT. •• SIX MILLION ACRES WITHIN THE "BLUE LINE" ARE NOW PROTECTED, NEARLY HALF STATE OWNED, COMPRISING THE LARGEST SUCH AREA EAST OF THE ROCKIES.

© MARTY POD SKOCH — SAM GLANZMAN 2004

VERPLANCK COLVIN
1847-1920

LYON MOUNTAIN STATION. COLVIN'S NORTHERNMOST HEADQUARTERS IN 1878. A FIRE-TOWER SITS HERE TODAY.

VERPLANCK COLVIN SUPERVISED THE SURVEYING AND MAPPING OF THE ADIRONDACK MOUNTAINS FROM 1872-1900. HUNDREDS OF TREES ON MOUNTAIN SUMMETS WERE FELLED TO BUILD TOWERS, SHELTERS AND SIGHT LINES THROUGH THE TREES. COLVIN INVENTED A "STAN-HELIO," A TIN DEVICE ATOP A SIGNAL TOWER, WHICH REFLECTED THE SUN. SURVEYORS ON ANOTHER SUMMIT USED A TRANSIT TO SPOT THE REFLECTION AND USED TRIANGULATION TO CALCULATE THE MOUNT-AIN'S ELEVATION. TODAY MANY SUMMITS SUCH AS BLUE, ST REGIS, AMPERSAND, HURRICANE AND PHARAOH ARE STILL TREELESS DUE TO HIS SURVEY.

© MARTY PODSKOCH — SAM GLANZMAN 2005

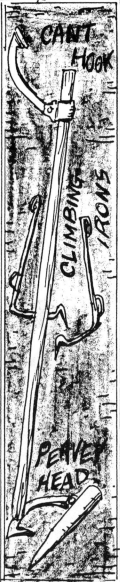

THE MID 19th CENTURY ADIRONDACK LOGGERS WERE A RUGGED GROUP OF MEN WHO WORKED FROM BEFORE DAWN TO NEAR DARK DEEP IN THE MOUNTAIN FOREST. IN THE MID 19th CENTURY A MAN GOT ABOUT 75 CENTS A DAY, PLUS ROOM AND BOARD, AND LIVED IN A CRUDE LOG BUNKHOUSE WITH HIS FELLOWS. THE LOGGING CAMP HAD A BLACKSMITH SHACK, AN OFFICE AND COMMISSARY. THE COOK WAS OFTEN THE HIGHEST PAID EMPLOYEE PREPARING A HEARTY BREAKFAST OF A DOZEN EGGS AND FLAPJACKS PER LOGGER AND LOTS OF COFFEE. AFTER FOURTEEN HRS. IN THE WOODS THE LOGGERS ATE IN SILENCE. THE MAIN INGREDIENT WAS BEANS, BUT THERE WAS ALSO BOILED EGGS, POTATOES, BREAD, SALT PORK, DONUTS, PIES, VENISON, AND SOMETIMES BEAR. AFTER DINNER THE MEN TOLD STORIES, SMOKED, SANG AND SHARPENED THEIR AXES.

© 2005

MARTY PODSKOCH
SAM GLANZMAN

CUTTING TREES

DURING MOST OF THE 1800s LOGGERS USED AN AXE TO FELL TREES. THE SHOUT OF "**TIMBER!**" WARNED OTHERS THAT A TREE WAS ABOUT TO FALL. CONTESTS WERE HELD TO SEE WHO COULD DROP A TREE ON A STAKE. ONCE A TREE WAS FELLED AND ITS LIMBS TRIMMED IT WAS CUT INTO 13-FOOT LENGTHS CALLED "MARKET LOGS." WORKING MOSTLY FROM OCTOBER TO APRIL, SIX DAYS A WEEK, AN AVERAGE MAN CUT 40 TREES A DAY. A GOOD CHOPPER CUT 50-70 A DAY, BUT THERE WERE A FEW MEN WHO CUT AS MANY AS 100 TREES IN A DAY. IN THE LATE 1880s AFTER LOGGERS BEGAN TO USE CROSSCUT SAWS TWO SKILLED WOODSMEN COULD CUT 100 TREES IN A DAY.

© 2005 - MARTY PODSKOCH - SAM GLANZMAN

LOG SKIDDING

AFTER A LUMBERJACK FELLED A TREE A TEAMSTER WITH A PAIR OF OXEN OR HORSES DREW THE LOGS TO A MOUNTAIN SKIDWAY. A TEAM OF OXEN HAD A LARGE IRON RING ATTACHED TO A HEAVY WOODEN YOKE. LOGS WERE ...

...CHAINED TOGETHER AND ATTACHED TO THE RING. THE TEAMS DREW THE LOGS TO THE UPPER END OF A SKID-WAY ON THE SIDE OF A HILL. LOGGERS USED A PIKE OR A PEAVEY TO ROLL THE LOGS ONTO THE PILE. A GOOD TEAMSTER COULD SKID BETWEEN 50-75 LOGS A DAY. THE LOGS WERE MOVED BY SLED TO BANKING GROUNDS FOR THE SPRING FLOODS.

© 2005
MARTY PODSKOCH
SAM GLANZMAN

SPRINKLER WAGON 1900

DURING THE WINTER ADIRONDACK LOGGERS CUT TREES AND USED HORSE DRAWN SLEDS TO BRING HEAVY LOADS OF LOGS OUT OF THE WOODS. FIRST, LIGHT LOADS OF LOGS WERE HAULED TO BREAK A TRACK AND THE ROAD MONKEYS BEGAN BUILDING ROADS. THEY USED SPRINKLER WAGONS TO ICE THE RUTS MADE BY SLEDS. MEN OPENED TWO HOLES BEHIND THE RUNNERS AND WATER DRIPPED IN THE RUTS AND FROZE. WORK — ERS FILLED THE TANKS WITH WATER FROM STREAMS OR WATER HOLES. SOME TANKS HELD FORTY BARRELS OF WATER. MEN BEGAN EARLY IN THE MORNING USING KEROSENE TORCHES OR LAN — TERNS TO GUIDE THEIR WAY.

© MARTY PODSKOCH — SAM GLANZMAN 2005

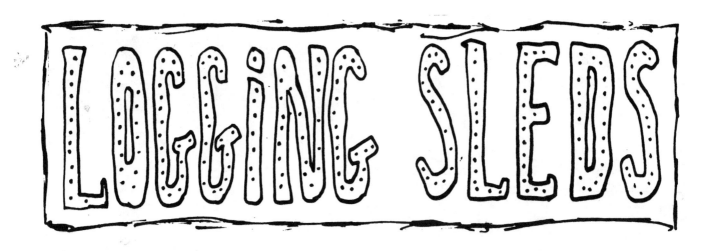

DURING THE WINTER, TEAMSTERS HAULED HUGE LOADS OF LOGS ON SLEDS FROM SKIDWAYS TO BANKING GROUNDS NEAR RIVERS OR LAKES. THESE SLEDS, WITH HEAVY WOODEN RUNNERS, CARRIED ENORMOUS LOADS HELD ON BY CHAINS. BEFORE DAWN TEAMSTERS SAT ATOP LOADS 10 TO 12 FEET HIGH AND DROVE A PAIR OF HORSES. ICY ROADS BECAME DANGEROUS ON STEEP HILLS. SOME DRIVERS JUMPED OFF IF THE SLED WENT TOO FAST! THE HORSES HAD TO RACE THE SLED TO THE BOTTOM. ON TREACHER-OUS HILLS, LOGGERS SECURED A BARIENGER BRAKE TO A STUMP AT THE TOP OF A HILL. A LINE FROM THE SLED WOUND AROUND THE 4-PULLEY BRAKE. BY PULLING ON LEVERS IT INCREASED BRAK-ING FRICTION AND EASED THE LOAD DOWN THE HILL.

CIRCA 1916

© 2005 MARTY POOSKOCH ~ SAM GLANZMAN

LOGGING

RIVER DRIVES

LOG DRIVING BEGAN IN THE ADIRONDACKS ABOUT 1813 ON THE SCHROON RIVER. LUMBERJACKS CUT THE PINE AND SPRUCE TREES DURING THE FALL AND WINTER AND DEPOSITED THE LOGS ALONG THE BANKS OF THE STREAMS. THEY RELEASED THE LOGS INTO THE SPRING RIVER RUNS. A RIVER DRIVER USED A PEAVY AND PIKE POLE TO KEEP THE LOGS MOVING WHILE SOME MEN STOOD WATCH AT BENDS IN THE BANKS OR ON BARS OR ISLANDS TO KEEP LOGS FROM JAMMING. OTHERS FOLLOWED THE DRIVE AND CLEARED THE SHORES. OFTEN, DRIVERS WERE INJURED OR KILLED. RIVER DRIVES ENDED AT LARGE CITIES SUCH AS PLATTSBURGH OR GLENS FALLS. THE LOGS WERE SEPARATED BY THEIR MARKS AND HAULED TO LUMBER AND PAPER MILLS. THE LAST DRIVES ENDED DURING THE 1940'S.

© MARTY PODSKOCH - SAM GLANZMAN 2005

BiG BooM

IN 1851 THE HUDSON RIVER BOOM ASSOCIATION FROM GLENS FALLS AREA BUILT THE "BIG BOOM" ACROSS THE HUDSON AT A SHARP TURN FOUR MILES NORTH OF GLENS FALLS. MASSIVE RAFTS OF CHAINED LOGS, ANCHORED BY "PIERS" MADE WITH 12 X 12 WHITE PINE TIMBERS FASTENED TOGETHER INTO A SQUARE SECTION ABOUT 24' LONG. SPRUCE, HEMLOCK AND PINE LOGS PILED UP TO 20' THICK BEHIND THE STURDY BOOM. LOGS, MARKED ON THE END BY THEIR OWNER, WERE COLLECTED, SORTED AND FLOATED TO MILLS. IN 1859 SPRING RAINS AND FLOOD BROKE THE BOOM, AND LOGS SHOT DOWN THE HUDSON RIVER TO AS FAR AS TROY. THE BOOM WAS REBUILT IN 1872 AND COLLECTED OVER A MILLION LOGS. IN 1922 THE LAST RIVER DRIVE WAS HELD.

©MARTY PODSKOCH 2005
SAM GLANZMAN

LINN TRACTORS

HOLMAN HARRY LINN PRODUCED FARM AND ROAD TRACTORS AND TRAILERS AT THE LINN MFG. CORP. (1917-1952) IN MORRIS, N.Y. THESE GASOLINE-POWERED VEHICLES WERE PROPELLED BY TRACKS IN THE REAR AND HAD STEERING RUNNERS IN THE FRONT. THEY COST ABOUT 4,500.00 DOLLARS, WEIGHED 4 TONS, WERE 25' X 7' HAD A 40 HP GAS ENGINE, COULD CARRY 5 TO 7 TON LOADS, AND DRAW 12 MORE TON ON SLEIGHS OR WAGONS. JOHN B. TODD, SUPERVISOR OF LOGGING OPERATIONS AT THE GOULD PAPER CO. OF LYON FALLS, CONVINCED HIS COMPANY TO BUY 3 LYON TRACTORS. HE SAID ONE LINN TRACTOR COULD HAUL AS MUCH AS 10 HORSE TEAMS. THE RAQUETTE LAKE SUPPLY CO. USED LINN TRACTORS 24-HOURS A DAY. LINNS CHANGED THE LOGGING INDUSTRY BECAUSE THEY HAULED LOGS DIRECTLY TO ROADSIDE LANDINGS, RAILROADS AND MILLS THUS ELIMINATING RIVER DRIVES.

© 2005 - MARTY PODSKOCH - SAM GLANZMAN

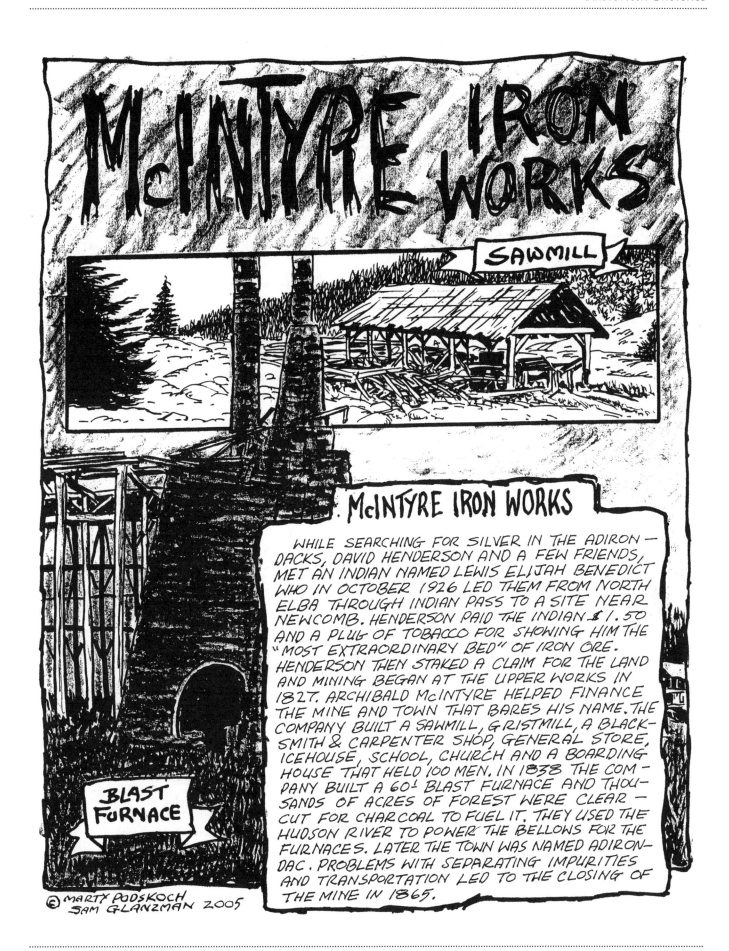

McINTYRE IRON WORKS

SAWMILL

BLAST FURNACE

McINTYRE IRON WORKS

WHILE SEARCHING FOR SILVER IN THE ADIRON-
DACKS, DAVID HENDERSON AND A FEW FRIENDS,
MET AN INDIAN NAMED LEWIS ELIJAH BENEDICT
WHO IN OCTOBER 1926 LED THEM FROM NORTH
ELBA THROUGH INDIAN PASS TO A SITE NEAR
NEWCOMB. HENDERSON PAID THE INDIAN $1.50
AND A PLUG OF TOBACCO FOR SHOWING HIM THE
"MOST EXTRAORDINARY BED" OF IRON ORE.
HENDERSON THEN STAKED A CLAIM FOR THE LAND
AND MINING BEGAN AT THE UPPER WORKS IN
1827. ARCHIBALD McINTYRE HELPED FINANCE
THE MINE AND TOWN THAT BARES HIS NAME. THE
COMPANY BUILT A SAWMILL, GRISTMILL, A BLACK-
SMITH & CARPENTER SHOP, GENERAL STORE,
ICEHOUSE, SCHOOL, CHURCH AND A BOARDING
HOUSE THAT HELD 100 MEN. IN 1838 THE COM-
PANY BUILT A 60¹ BLAST FURNACE AND THOU-
SANDS OF ACRES OF FOREST WERE CLEAR-
CUT FOR CHARCOAL TO FUEL IT. THEY USED THE
HUDSON RIVER TO POWER THE BELLOWS FOR THE
FURNACES. LATER THE TOWN WAS NAMED ADIRON-
DAC. PROBLEMS WITH SEPARATING IMPURITIES
AND TRANSPORTATION LED TO THE CLOSING OF
THE MINE IN 1865.

© MARTY PODSKOCH
SAM GLANZMAN 2005

CALAMITY POND
CALAMITY BROOK

CALAMITY POND AND CALAMITY BROOK ARE SO-NAMED BECAUSE OF THE TRAGIC ACCIDENTAL SHOOTING OF DAVID HENDERSON AT THAT PLACE ON SEPT. 3, 1845. HENDERSON, AN ADMINISTRATOR OF THE McINTYRE IRON CO. NEAR NEWCOMB, WAS LOOKING FOR A WAY TO GET MORE WATER TO POWER THE MIGHTY BELLOWS THAT FANNED THE FLAMES AT THE MILL. THE MILL WAS ON THE HUDSON RIVER IN ITS EARLY STAGES AND MORE POWER WAS NEEDED.

HENDERSON THOUGHT IT POSSIBLE TO DIVERT THE OPALESCENT RIVER INTO THE HUDSON, PROVIDING VOLUME. HIS GUIDE, JOHN CHENEY, HIS SON, AND TWO OTHERS WERE WITH HENDERSON WHEN THEY CAME UPON DUCKS SITTING ON A POND. IT WAS AT THAT FATEFUL SPOT, HENDERSON'S GUN UNEXPECTEDLY WENT OFF, KILLING HIM. HIS LAST WORDS WERE: "THIS IS A HORRIBLE PLACE FOR A MAN TO DIE." HIS SONS ERECTED A MONUMENT TO HIS MEMORY NEAR THE FATEFUL SPOT.

© MARTY PODSKOCH — SAM GLANZMAN 2005

MINEVILLE IRON MINES

MINEVILLE (NW OF PORT HENRY ON LAKE CHAMPLAIN) WAS HOME TO ONE OF THE WORLD'S LARGEST IRON ORE DEPOSITS IN THE 19TH CENTURY. MINING BEGAN IN 1804 AND CONTINUED FOR OVER 150 YEARS. AT FIRST OPEN PITS WERE USED, THEN EXTENSIVE TUNNELING USING HAND DRILLS AND BLACK POWDER WENT TO 315' DEEP BY 1852. IN 1952 TUNNELS WERE 3500' DEEP. THE ORE WAS SENT TO LAKE CHAMPLAIN WHERE IT WAS SHIPPED TO FURNACES ON THE EAST COAST.

MINEVILLE IRON WAS USED TO SHEATH THE U.S.S. MONITOR DURING THE CIVIL WAR.

Sketch plan Published 1862

IN THE LATE 1800s WITHERBEE AND SHERMAN CO. HIRED IMMIGRANTS FROM EUROPE AND CANADA, WHO WORKED 10-12 HOURS, SIX DAYS A WEEK ARRIVING AT 5:30 RIDING CAGE ELEVATORS TO GREAT DEPTHS, AND SOMETIMES WALKING UNDERGROUND ONE AND A HALF HOURS TO WORK. BY 1905 13,000,000 TONS OF ORE HAD BEEN REMOVED. REPUBLIC STEEL RAN THE MINES FROM 1942 TILL IT CLOSED IN 1961. THERE IS AN IRON CENTER MUSEUM IN PORT HENRY.

CHARCOAL KILNS

A CHARCOAL MAKER RESTING, CIRCA 1889 AND A CHARCOAL KILN.

CHARCOAL KILNS WERE USED IN THE EARLY PRODUCTION OF IRON IN THE ADIRONDACKS. THE HUGE KILNS HELD MOSTLY HARDWOODS STACKED ABOUT 20' DEEP AND COVERED WITH EARTH OR SOD, SET AFIRE, AND KEPT SMOLDERING FOR UP TO TWO WEEKS. BRICK BEEHIVE KILNS HAD A LARGE OPENING ON THE TOP AND THREE OPENINGS NEAR THE BOTTOM. ONE CORD OF WOOD MADE 30 TO 35 BUSHELS OF CHARCOAL. IT TOOK 600 BUSHELS TO MAKE 1 TON OF IRON FROM 4 TONS OF ORE. IN 1864 30 ADIRONDACK FORGES CONSUMED ABOUT 6,700,000 BUSHELS OF CHARCOAL. THE CHATEAUGAY ORE & IRON CO. CUT 2,000 ACRES A YEAR FOR ITS 70 KILNS. BY 1900 ABOUT 250,000 ACRES HAD BEEN CLEAR-CUT TO MAKE CHARCOAL FOR THE IRON INDUSTRY.

FLUE →

CORD WOOD →

TO MAKE CHARCOAL, A CIRCULAR AREA (HEARTH) IS LEVELED, COVERED WITH SLABS OF WOOD AND BARK. A FLUE IS ERECTED WITH EITHER POLES OR STACKED LOGS. CORD WOOD IS STACKED AROUND THE FLUE. THE WOODPILE IS THAN COVERED WITH DIRT AND WET LEAVES, THAN SET AFIRE

© MARTY PODSKOCH - SAM GLANZMAN 2004

BENSON MINES

BENSON MINES, EAST OF STAR LAKE IN SOUTH ST. LAWRENCE CO., WAS ONE OF THE LARGEST OPEN-PIT IRON MAGNETITE ORE MINES IN THE WORLD. IN 1810 US ARMY ENGINEERS SURVEYING A ROAD FROM ALBANY TO OGDENSBURG DISCOVERED ORE WHEN THEIR COMPASSES STOPPED POINTING NORTH. MANY COMPANIES MINED THERE: CLIFTON IRON (1866-1870), MAGNETIC IRON (1889-1893), BENSON MINES (1907-1919). WORKING CONDITIONS WERE EXTREMELY HAZARDOUS. ONE EXPLOSION IN 1908 SCATTERED FOUR MEN OVER 100'. STEAM DRILLS AND EXPLOSIVES LOOSENED THE ROCK, LOADED BY STEAM SHOVELS INTO RAILROAD CARS AND CRUSHER AND SEPARATED IN A PROCESSING PLANT, HEATED IN HUGE KILNS, POURED INTO NODULES, AND SHIPPED TO STEEL PLANTS IN PA. THE TOWN HAD NINE SALOONS EACH A SOURCE OF ENTERTAINMENT FOR THE MINERS AND LOGGERS. THE LAST OWNER, JONES AND LAUGHLIN STEEL CO., EMPLOYER ABOUT 800 PEOPLE WORKING IN AN OPEN PIT GASH IN THE HILLS OVER 2 MILES LONG. ALTHOUGH THE MINE CLOSED IN 1978, THE LAND BEARS AN UGLY SCAR, ABANDONED BUILDINGS DECAY, MOUNTAINS OF WASTE (TAILINGS) TOWER OVER THE ENORMOUS PIT FILLED WITH STAGNANT WATER.

Benson Mines, N.Y., ca. 1915

© 2008 MARTY PODSKOCH SAM GLANZMAN

BARTON MINES

IN 1878 HENRY HUDSON BARTON SR. BEGAN MINING GARNETS FROM AN OPEN PIT MINE NEAR NORTH CREEK AND USED THE HARD RED STONE TO MAKE SANDPAPER. MINERS USED HORSE DRAWN CARTS AND PICK AXES IN THE MINING OPERATION. THEY SEPARATED THE GARNET CRYSTALS, WHICH VARIED IN SIZE FROM A FEW OUNCES TO FIFTY POUNDS, FROM THE WASTE ROCK. AS THE DEMAND FOR GARNET INCREASED, MINING OPERATIONS PROGRESSED. ELECTRICITY AND ROADWAYS WERE ESTABLISHED AND IN 1924, A PLANT ON GORE MOUNTAIN WAS BUILT USING MORE MODERN MILLING METHODS TO CRUSH, SEPARATE AND GRADE THE GARNET CRYSTALS.
OPERATION OF THE MINE CEASED IN 1983 AND RELOCATED TO RUBY MOUNTAIN, SOME 4 MILES TO THE NORTHEAST. TODAY, THE BARTON MINES COMPANY PRODUCES INDUSTRIAL ABRASIVES FOR WATERJET CUTTING, SURFACE PREPARATION, COATINGS REMOVAL AND OTHER SPECIALIZED APPLICATIONS. GARNET IS ALSO N.Y STATE'S GEMSTONE.

©2005 MARTY PODSKOCH ~ SAM GLANZMAN

THE MILL IN GRAPHITE — MID 1900

GRAPHITE, A SMALL COMMUNITY WEST OF HAGUE ON LAKE GEORGE, HAD ONE OF THE WORLD'S PUREST DEPOSITS OF GRAPHITE. IN 1887 SAM AKERMAN DISCOVERED THE SOFT BLACK LUSTROUS CARBON THAT CONDUCTS ELECTRICITY AND IS USED IN PENCILS AS A LUBRICANT. THE AMERICAN GRAPHITE CO. BEGAN EXTRACTION IN AN OPEN PIT AND THEN DUG 1½ MILES OF TUNNELS. MINERS EARNED A DIME AN HOUR BLASTING AND DIGGING. MANY BECAME SICK, MANY DIED FROM THE DUST AND EXPLOSIONS. DURING THE WINTER, WORKERS TRANSPORTED UP TO 2-TON LOADS ON HORSE-DRAWN SLEDS DOWN THE HILL TO LAKE GEORGE TO BE PUT ON BARGES HEADED FOR THE PROCESSING PLANT IN TICONDEROGA FOR MAKING PENCILS. IN 1891 A 5-STORY PROCESSING MILL (100' X 500'), BUILT IN GRAPHITE, WAS POWERED BY A WOOD FURNACE THAT USED 10 CORDS OF FOUR FOOT LOGS A DAY. THE TOWN OF GRAPHITE GREW UP NEAR THE MINE WITH ITS OWN SCHOOL, CHURCH, POST OFFICE, STORE AND THREE SALOONS. THE MINE CLOSED IN THE EARLY 1920s. TODAY THE ABANDONED TUNNELS ARE THE WINTER HOME OF ABOUT 200,000 BATS.

© MARTY PODSKOCH — 2006
SAM GLANZMAN

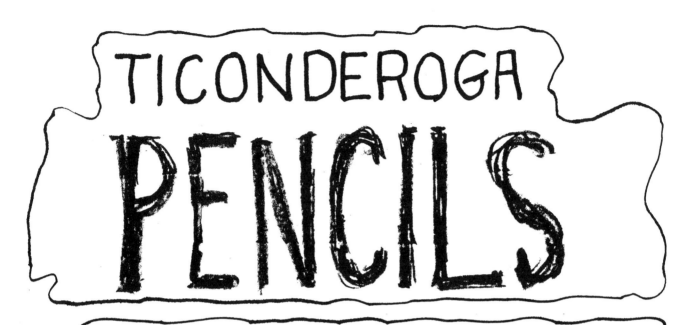

TICONDEROGA PENCILS

A WOODEN PENCIL FILLED WITH GRAPHITE WAS INVENTED IN THE TICONDEROGA AREA AROUND 1830. THE GRAPHITE HAD BEEN DIS-COVERED IN 1815 IN CHILSON WEST OF TICONDEROGA. GUY C. BALDWIN, A LOCAL INVENTOR, REFINED THE GRAPHITE AND IN 1833 RECEIVED A PATENT FOR A GRAPHITE PENCIL. PEOPLE STILL USED A QUILL PEN AND INK FOR WRITING BUT DURING THE CIVIL WAR DEMAND INCREASED FOR A PORTABLE, CLEAN AND DRY WRITING TOOL. THE JOSEPH DIXON CRUCIBLE CO. BEGAN TO MASS PRODUCE PENCILS USING GRAPHITE FROM ITS MINE IN HAGUE NEAR LAKE GEORGE. IT WAS PROCESSED IN TICONDEROGA AND SHIPPED TO JERSEY CITY, NJ, WHERE IT WAS MIXED WITH CLAY POWDER AND WATER AND MADE INTO A SPA-GHETTI-LIKE STRING THAT WAS HARDENED IN A KILN AND INSERT-ED BETWEEN TWO GROOVED PIECES OF WOOD THAT WERE GLUED TOGETHER AND VARNISHED OR PAINTED. IN 1872 THE DIXON COMPA-NY MADE 86,000 PENCILS A DAY AND BY 1892 HAD MANUFACTURED OVER 30 MILLION. IN 1913 THE COMPANY NAMED ITS PENCIL THE 'DIXON-TICONDEROGA' AFTER THE REVOLUTIONARY FORT. TODAY, PEOPLE AROUND THE WORLD WRITE WITH A DIXON-TICONDEROGA PENCIL.

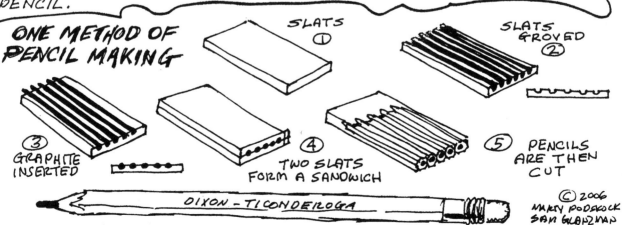

ONE METHOD OF PENCIL MAKING

SLATS ①

SLATS GROVED ②

③ GRAPHITE INSERTED

④ TWO SLATS FORM A SANDWICH

⑤ PENCILS ARE THEN CUT

DIXON - TICONDEROGA

© 2006
MARTY PODSKOCH
SAM GLANZMAN

TITANIUM IN M.INTYRE MINE

THE McINTYRE IRON MINE IN TAHAWUS NEAR NEWCOMB WAS CLOSED IN 1857 BECAUSE THE IRON ORE CONTAINED IMPURITIES, INCLUDING, ILMENITE USED TO MAKE TITANIUM OXIDE. IN THE EARLY 1900s METHODS WERE DEVELOPED TO EXTRACT TITANIUM, A LIGHTWEIGHT, HIGH-STRENGTH, LOW-CORROSION METAL. IN 1941 THE NATIONAL LEAD CORPORATION (NLC) ACQUIRED THE McINTYRE MINE PROPERTY AND USED NEW METHODS TO EXTRACT THE IRON AND TITANIUM....

.... THE US GOVERNMENT BUILT A RAILROAD SPUR TO THE NLC MINE TO TRANSPORT THE MINERALS USED FOR WWII. TITANIUM DIOXIDE WAS DISPENSED FROM AIRCRAFT AND WAR SHIPS TO CREATE A VERTICAL SMOKE SCREEN. NLC CLOSED THE TAHAWUS MINE IN THE 1980s AFTER EXTRACTING ALMOST 100 MILLION TONS OF TITANIUM. TITANIUM IS USED TODAY IN PAINT PIGMENTS, AIRCRAFT, AEROSPACE, AUTOMOBILES, PROSTHETICS, JEWELRY, AND SPORTING GOODS.

2006 ©MARTY PODSKOCH - SAM GLANZMAN

TANNERIES
HEMLOCK BARK

HEMLOCK BARK WAS HARVESTED FROM ABOUT A MILLION ACRES OF TREES IN THE ADIRONDACKS DURING THE MID-TO LATE-19TH CENTURY TO PROVIDE TANNIN, ESSENTIAL IN MAKING LEATHER. DURING THE 1850'S MORE THAN 150 TANNERIES POPPED UP ALL AROUND THE ADIRONDACK PARK AND TOWNS GREW UP AROUND THEM. CORDUROY ROADS RADIATED OUT INTO THE VIRGIN FORESTS. WHEN THE SAP WAS FLOWING IN THE SPRING AND EARLY SUMMER, BARK PEELERS CUT A 'BUTT' RING AT THE BASE OF A TREE AND ANOTHER RING 4-FEET HIGHER. A 2-FOOT, SPOON-SHAPED BLADE CALLED A 'SPUDDER' CARVED A 1-FOOT-WIDE PIECE BETWEEN THE TWO CUTS. THE TREE WAS THEN FELLED AND ALL THE BARK WAS REMOVED. WORKERS STACKED THE BARK AND TEAMSTERS HAULED IT ON WAGONS AND SLEDS. THE BARK FROM ONE TREE WOULD TAN ONE HIDE! PEELERS LIVED IN ROUGH HUTS AND WERE PAID ABOUT $2.00 A DAY PLUS BOARD. LIKE THE SLAUGHTERED BUFFALO ON THE PLAINS, THE TREES WERE OFTEN LEFT TO ROT.

©2006 MARTY PODSKOCH
SAM GLANZMAN

TANNERIES

TANNING LEATHER WAS A VITAL INDUSTRY IN THE ADIRONDACKS BETWEEN 1850-1880. THERE WERE MORE THAN 150 TANNERIES MOST IN REMOTE AREAS IN OR NEAR THE ADIRONDACK PARK ADJACENT TO HEMLOCK FORESTS THAT YIELDED 'TANNIN.' HIDES FROM SOUTH AND CENTRAL AMERICA AND THE AMERICAN WEST WERE TRANSPORTED TO NYC AND THEN BY WATER AND WAGONS TO THE TANNERIES. TEAMSTERS HAULED THOUSANDS OF CORDS OF HEMLOCK BARK AND STACKED THEM IN BARN-SIZE PILES. TANNING TOOK PLACE IN ONE LARGE BUILDING OR IN MULTIPLE BUILDINGS THAT INCLUDED A BEAM HOUSE, A LEACH OR VAT HOUSE, A STEAM HOUSE, DRYING SHEDS, AND FINISHING ROOMS. WHOLE TOWNS GREW UP NEAR TANNERIES WHERE MANY IMMIGRANTS WORKED FOR LOW PAY IN FOUL CONDITIONS. EACH TANNERY CURED 30-70,000 HIDES A YEAR FOR SOLES, HARNESSES, MILITARY EQUIPMENT, AND INDUSTRIAL BELTING. AFTER 1880, ADIRONDACK TANNERIES BEGAN TO CLOSE, AS OTHERS OPENED NEAR SLAUGHTERHOUSES IN THE MID-WEST AND NEW SHOE FACTORIES IN THE SOUTHERN TIER OF NEW YORK.

TEAMSTER HAULING BARK

© 2006 MARTY POUSKOCH - SAM GLANZMAN

TANNING HIDES

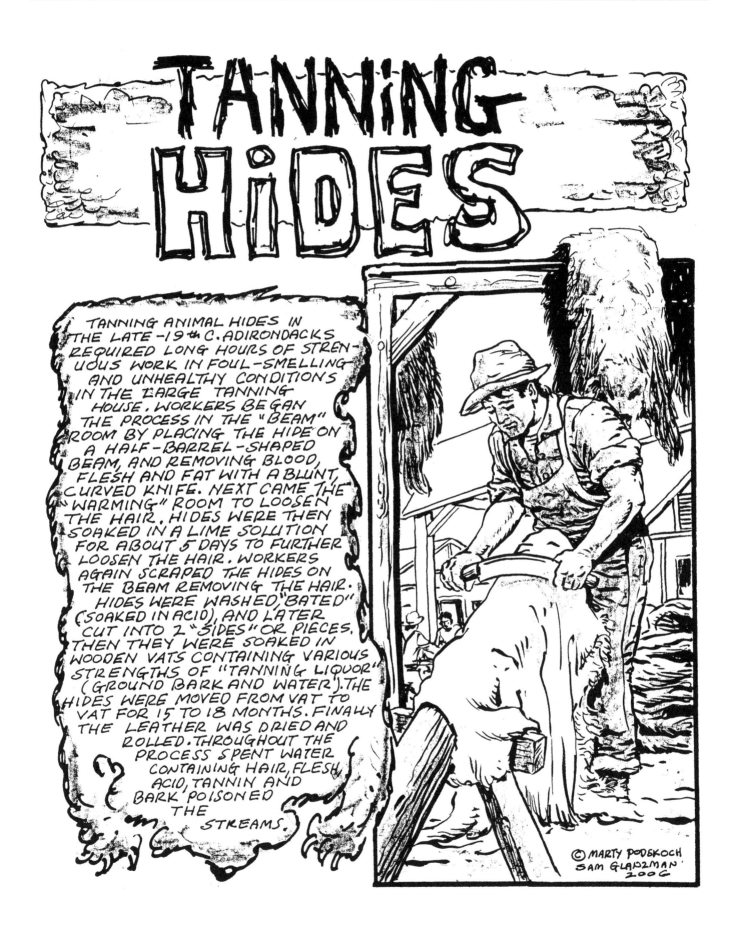

TANNING ANIMAL HIDES IN THE LATE -19th C. ADIRONDACKS REQUIRED LONG HOURS OF STRENUOUS WORK IN FOUL-SMELLING AND UNHEALTHY CONDITIONS IN THE LARGE TANNING HOUSE. WORKERS BEGAN THE PROCESS IN THE "BEAM" ROOM BY PLACING THE HIDE ON A HALF-BARREL-SHAPED BEAM, AND REMOVING BLOOD, FLESH AND FAT WITH A BLUNT, CURVED KNIFE. NEXT CAME THE "WARMING" ROOM TO LOOSEN THE HAIR. HIDES WERE THEN SOAKED IN A LIME SOLUTION FOR ABOUT 5 DAYS TO FURTHER LOOSEN THE HAIR. WORKERS AGAIN SCRAPED THE HIDES ON THE BEAM REMOVING THE HAIR.
    HIDES WERE WASHED, "BATED" (SOAKED IN ACID), AND LATER CUT INTO 2 "SIDES" OR PIECES. THEN THEY WERE SOAKED IN WOODEN VATS CONTAINING VARIOUS STRENGTHS OF "TANNING LIQUOR" (GROUND BARK AND WATER). THE HIDES WERE MOVED FROM VAT TO VAT FOR 15 TO 18 MONTHS. FINALLY THE LEATHER WAS DRIED AND ROLLED. THROUGHOUT THE PROCESS SPENT WATER CONTAINING HAIR, FLESH ACID, TANNIN AND BARK POISONED THE STREAMS.

© MARTY PODSKOCH
SAM GLANZMAN
2006

SPRUCE
GUM PICKERS

EASTERN SPRUCES OF THE COOL NORTHERN FORESTS —

BLACK SPRUCE

WHITE SPRUCE

RED SPRUCE

SPRUCE RESIN WAS THE FIRST COMMERCIAL GUM IN AMERICA. COLONISTS LEARNED TO CHEW SPRUCE SAP FROM THE INDIANS. FROM ABOUT 1880 TO 1915 GUM PICKERS SPENT WEEKS IN THE ADIRONDACK FORESTS GATHERING SPRUCE SAP TO SUPPLE- MENT THEIR INCOME. THEY SOLD THE AMBER RESIN TO DRUGGISTS AND CHEWING COMPANIES. PEOPLE CARRIED THE MEDICINAL-TASTING, BUT RE- FRESHING BALLS OF RESIN IN SMALL WOOD- EN BOXES. THE RESIN WAS ALSO USED ON CUTS AND RASHES AND IN A BROTH FOR COLDS. SPRUCE RESIN OOZED FROM A CUT IN THE TREE BARK. GUMMERS HARVESTED THE "HEALING SALVE OF THE TREE," BY SCRAPING IT OFF WITH A BLADE ATTACHED TO A LONG STICK. THE GUM FELL INTO A CAN OR BAG. PICKERS COLLECTED ABOUT 10 POUNDS A DAY, BUT TIM CROWLEY OF PISECO ONCE GATHERED 100 POUNDS IN A DAY.

© 2005 MARTY PODSKOCH – SAM GLANZMAN

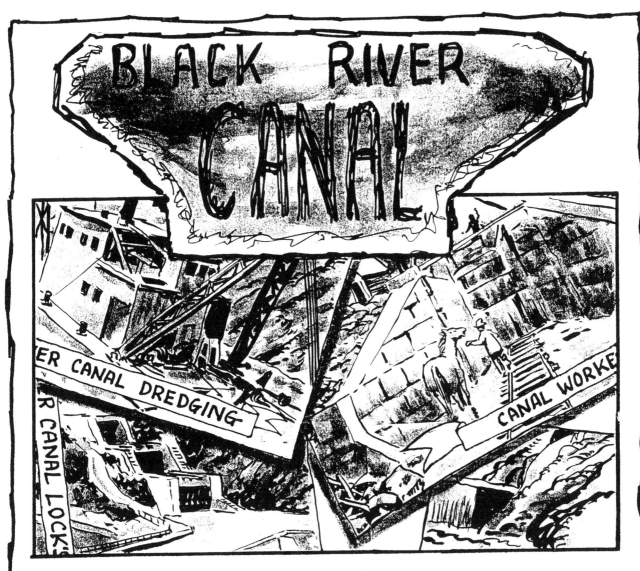

THE BLACK RIVER CANAL, COMPLETED IN 1851, RAN 35 MILES FROM THE ERIE CANAL AT ROME, NY TO THE BLACK RIVER AT HIGH FALLS (LYONS FALLS). IT HAD 109 LOCKS TO LIFT THE BOATS AND WATER NEARLY 1100 FEET. RESIDENTS OF LEWIS COUNTY URGED THE STATE TO BUILD THE CANAL TO TRANSPORT THEIR, TIMBER, IRON ORE, AND FARM GOODS TO EAST COAST MARKETS. IN THE PAST GOODS HAD TO BE TRANSPORTED ABOUT 2,000 MILES DOWN THE BLACK RIVER TO LAKE ONTARIO, THEN ON THE ST. LAWRENCE RIVER, AND FINALLY THE NORTH ATLANTIC TO NYC. WITH THE CANAL IT WAS ONLY ABOUT 250 MILES. THERE WAS EVEN REGULAR PASSENGER SERVICE FROM LYONS FALLS TO CARTHAGE. IT WAS ALSO NAVIGABLE FOR STEAMBOATS, IN 1897 NEAR FORESTPORT 400' OF THE TOWPATH WASHED OUT AND 1,700 MEN WORKED 30 DAYS TO REPAIR IT. THE CANAL DECLINED IN USE DUE TO RAILROAD COMPETITION AND DEPLETION OF NATURAL RESOURCES AND CLOSED IN 1924. REMNANTS OF ITS LOCKS ARE STILL VISIBLE.

© 2005 MARTY PODSKOCH ~ SAM GLANZMAN

"DR. WEBB'S RAILROAD"

THE CENTRAL ADIRONDACKS WAS AN ISOLATED WILDERNESS UNTIL DR. WILLIAM SEWARD WEBB FINANCED THE BUILDING OF A RAILROAD FROM HERKIMER TO MALONE. HE MARRIED INTO THE VANDERBILT FAMILY AND WAS PRESIDENT OF THE WAGNER PALACE CAR, LATER THE PULLMAN CO. IN 1891 CONSTRUCTION WORKERS CUT THROUGH DENSE VIRGIN FOREST AND MOUNTAINS, BUILT BRIDGES, AND LAID 200 MILES OF TRACK IN LESS THAN 20 MONTHS. THE MOHAWK AND MALONE RAILROAD (ADIRONDACK AND ST. LAWRENCE LINE) BROUGHT THOUSANDS TO ENJOY RECREATIONAL AND HEALTH-GENERATING OPPORTUNITIES. TWO DECADES OF PROSPERITY FOLLOWED.

MALONE JUNCTION, N.Y. 1890s

THE STATION BUILDING WAS CONVERTED INTO A RESTAURANT/BAR DURING THE 1970s AND HAS SINCE BEEN MADE INTO A DOCTOR'S OFFICE. AS SUCH IT IS STILL STANDING TODAY.

© MARTY PODSKOCH – SAM GLANZMAN 2004

1900 · MARION RIVER CARRY RAILROAD · 1929

THE MARION RIVER CARRY RAILROAD WAS THE SHORTEST STANDARD-GAUGE RAILROAD IN THE WORLD, TRAVERSING A MERE 1300 YARDS PORTAGE (THE FORMER BASSET'S CARRY) IN THE LINE OF SMALL STEAMSHIPS TRANSPORTING TOURISTS AND CAMP OWNERS FROM RAQUETTE LAKE TO THE MARION RIVER TO UTOWANA LAKE AND ON TO BLUE MOUNTAIN LAKE. THE LINE WAS BUILT BY W.W. DURANT, PRESIDENT OF THE ADIRONDACK R.R. AT FIRST A SMALL LOCOMOTIVE PROVED UNABLE TO HAUL THE 3 OPEN STREETCARS FROM THE BROOKLYN TRANSIT COMPANY -- 1 BAGGAGE AND 2 PASSENGER CARS WITH A CAPACITY OF 125. A LARGER ENGINE WAS TOO HEAVY FOR THE ROADBED, SO A VERY SMALL LOCOMOTIVE, NUMBER 2 FROM THE H.K. PORTER CO. OF PITTSBURGH, BEGAN OPERATION IN AUGUST 1901. THIS ENGINE WAS STILL IN OPERATION IN 1929 WHEN THE ADVENT OF ROUTE 28 MADE ACCESS TO THE AREA MUCH EASIER.

© 2005 MARTY PODSKOCH

DR. THOMAS C. DURANT
AND
THE ADIRONDACK R.R.

DEPOT AT NORTH CREEK

DR. THOMAS CLARK DURANT (1820-85) HELPED OPEN THE CENTRAL ADIRONDACKS TO TOURISM. HE LEFT MEDICINE AND BECAME A SUCCESSFUL RAILROAD BUSINESSMAN. AS GENERAL MANAGER OF THE UNION PACIFIC RAILROAD IN 1869 HE DROVE THE LAST SPIKE OF THE TRANSCONTINENTAL RAILROAD. IN 1863, AS PRESIDENT OF THE ADIRONDACK RAILWAY CO., HE ACQUIRED 250,000 ACRES AT FIVE CENTS AN ACRE. DURANT WANTED TO TRANSPORT LOGS FROM HIS LAND AND BRING IN MORE TOURISTS. HE PROMISED THE STATE HE'D LAY 185 MILES OF TRACK FROM SARATOGA SPRINGS TO OGDENSBURG IF HIS LAND WAS TAX FREE TILL 1883. IN 1865 HE BEGAN CONSTRUCTION AND BY 1871 TRACK RAN 60 MILES TO NORTH CREEK. ALTHOUGH THE RAILROAD WASN'T COMPLETED, DURANT AND HIS SON, WILLIAM W., CREATED A RELIABLE TRANSPORTATION SYSTEM THAT OPENED THE CENTRAL ADIRONDACKS AND BROUGHT THOUSANDS OF TOURISTS BY STAGE COACH AND BOAT TO HOTELS AND CAMPS. DR. DURANT AMASSED ABOUT 670,000 ACRES OF LAND.
HE MADE NORTH CREEK HIS HOME WHERE HE DIED IN 1885. IN 1889 THE RAILROAD BECAME THE ADIRONDACK BRANCH OF THE DELAWARE AND HUDSON RAILROAD.

OWNEY THE MAIL DOG

IN 1888 A PUPPY WANDERED INTO THE POST OFFICE IN ALBANY AND FELL ASLEEP ON A MAILBAG. ONE POSTAL WORKER ASKED, "DOES ANY-ONE 'OWN' YOU?" THEY FED AND ADOPTED HIM AND CALLED HIM 'OWN-EY.' ONCE HE FOLLOWED HIS POSTAL BAG ONTO A TRAIN. AT THE NEXT STATION, WORKERS RETURNED HIM TO ALBANY. OWNEY MADE MANY TRIPS TO ADIRONDACK RAILROAD STATIONS AND MONTREAL. RAILWAY MAIL CLERKS ADOPTED OWNEY AND MARKED HIS TRAVELS BY PLACING MEDALS AND TAGS ON HIS COLLAR AND LATER ON HIS SWEATER-LIKE HARNESS. OWNEY EVENTUALLY TRAVELED THROUGHOUT THE U.S. EVEN THOUGH THERE WERE ABOUT 400 TRAIN WRECKS A YEAR, THE TRAIN THAT OWNEY WAS RIDING WAS ALWAYS SAFE. IN AUGUST 1895 HE BEGAN A FOUR-MONTH TRIP AROUND THE WORLD ON TRAINS AND SHIPS. TRAGEDY OC-CURRED IN 1897 WHEN OWNEY WAS MYSTERIOUSLY SHOT IN TOLEDO. HIS BODY HAS BEEN PRESERVED IN THE NATIONAL POSTAL MUSEUM IN WASHINGTON DC WEARING MANY OF HIS TAGS AND MEDALS.

© 2005 - MARTY PODSKOCH - SAM GLANZMAN

CYRUS COMSTOCK'S BUCKBOARD WAGON

CYRUS COMSTOCK (1765-1853), A CONGREGATIONALIST MINISTER, CREATED WHAT WAS ARGUABLY THE FIRST BUCKBOARD WAGON. HE SETTLED IN LEWIS, ESSEX CO. IN HIS EARLY 50'S AND TRAVELED YEAR-ROUND THROUGH THE PARISH HELPING THE POOR AND HUNGRY AND BRINGING THE CHURCH TO ISOLATED FARMS AND VILLAGES. HE WAS WELL-LOVED BY HIS FLOCK, OFTEN SLEEPING IN THEIR CRUDE CABINS AND SOME-TIMES WAKING COVERED WITH SNOW. TRAVELING FROM PLACE TO PLACE OVER ROUGH MOUNTAIN ROADS WAS OFTEN VERY PAINFUL. COMSTOCK DE-VELOPED AN OPEN, FOUR-WHEELED CARRIAGE WITH THE AXLES CONNECTED BY A FLEXIBLE BOARD. HE ATTACHED A SEAT(S) TO THE BOARD WHICH ACTED AS A SPRING GIVING A MORE COMFORTABLE RIDE. HIS DESIGN SPREAD THROUGHOUT THE ADIRONDACKS AND BEYOND. IRONICALLY, REV. COMSTOCK DIED IN AN ACCIDENT RIDING A BUCKBOARD NEAR WILLSBORO FALLS.

©2006
MARTY PODSKOCH
SAM GLANZMAN

BUCKBOARD

ADIRONDACK STAGECOACH LINES

1855   1900

BETWEEN 1855-1900 ADIRONDACK STAGECOACH LINES TRANSPORTED PEOPLE, PARCELS, AND MAIL FROM RAILROAD AND LAKE TERMINALS TO REMOTE HAMLETS IN THE WILDERNESS. TEAMSTERS DROVE 4-6 HORSE TEAMS OVER MUDDY, NARROW, BUMPY, ROADS UP TO 40 MILES A DAY IN ALL TYPES OF WEATHER AND OFTEN IN DARKNESS. DRIVERS WOULD YELL FOR PASSENGERS TO LEAN RIGHT OR LEFT ON SHARP CURVES. GEORGE MESERVE, A MASTERFUL DRIVER FOR PAUL SMITH'S HOTEL, CARRIED 3367 PASSENGERS FROM BLOOMINGDALE TO THE HOTEL WITHOUT AN ACCIDENT IN OVER 10 YEARS. WIELDING A 16 FOOT WHIP HE COULD FLICK A FLY OFF THE HEAD OF HIS LEAD HORSE. DURING THE DAY, SMITH'S DRIVERS DROVE 6 WHITE HORSES AND AT NIGHT 6 BLACK HORSES. SOME COACHES HELD NINE PASSENGERS INSIDE THE COACH AND UP TO TWELVE ON TOP. THE PERSON RIDING 'SHOTGUN' PAID EXTRA. AS THE SPEEDING COACH NEARED A STATION, A TRIUMPHANT HORN BLAST FROM THE DRIVER SIGNALED ITS ARRIVAL.

NEWCOMB SNOWPLOW AND ROLLER COMPANY

IN THE LATE 1800s JOHN ANDERSON JR., A LUMBERING BARON AND STORE OWNER IN NEWCOMB (ESSEX COUNTY), STARTED THE NEWCOMB SNOWPLOW AND ROLLER COMPANY. HIS FACTORY MADE HUGE WOODEN ROLLERS THAT WERE PULLED BY TWO TEAMS OF HORSES...

... IN THE FRONT OF THE ROLLER THERE WAS A DRIVER'S SEAT AND AN ADJUSTABLE PLOW. A SCRAPER BLADE KEPT THE WOODEN DRUM CLEAN AND A LEVELER ATTACHMENT DISTRIBUTED THE SNOW EVENLY. THE ROLLER COMPACTED THE SNOW FOR HORSE-DRAWN CUTTERS AND SLEDS. THE COMPANY ALSO MADE THE ANDERSON-GRIMES SNOWPLOW NAMED AFTER THE OWNER AND HIS HEAD MECHANIC AND SUPERVISOR OF THE PLANT, HOWARD GRIMES. THE PLOW COULD BREAK A 14-FT WIDE SWATH IN ANY DEPTH OF SNOW WHERE A TEAM COULD FIND FOOTING. NEWCOMB NATIVE SAMUEL JOHNSON IMPROVED THIS PLOW BY ADDING ADJUSTABLE WINGS. ON JANUARY 10, 1918, ANDERSON'S SNOW ROLLER AND PLOW FACTORY, GARAGE, BLACKSMITH SHOP, STORE, AND WAGON SHOP BURNED.

© 2006 - MARTY POUSKOCH - SAM GLANZMAN

FIRST MAILBOAT

© MARTY POUSIE·CH – SAM GIANZANA~ 2006

THE FIRST MAILBOAT IN THE U.S. BEGAN SERVICE IN 1901 TO SUMMER RESIDENTS ON THE FIRST FOUR LAKES OF THE FULTON CHAIN BECAUSE PRESIDENT BENJAMIN HARRISON (1889–93) HAD A SUMMER WHITE HOUSE ON SECOND LAKE. HE GOT CONGRESS TO AUTHORIZE THE MAIL ROUTE. FROM 1901–29, THE FULTON NAVIGATION CO. DELIVERED MAIL 7 DAYS A WEEK FROM JUNE 1ST TO OCTOBER 1ST AND ALSO CARRIED PASSENGERS. ITS FIRST STEAMER, "ZIP," COLLIDED WITH A BOAT AND SANK. IT WAS RAISED, REBUILT AND RENAMED "OLD FORGE." THE MAILBOAT WAS A POST OFFICE ON WATER. A CLERK SORTED IN-COMING MAIL AND AS THE BOAT PASSED A DOCK, HE LEANED OUT, HANDED A MAILBAG TO THE RESIDENT AND TOOK THE OUTGOING MAIL. THERE WAS ONE CLERK, SADLY WHO FELL WHEN THE RESTRAINING ROPE BROKE, HIT HIS HEAD ON THE DOCK AND DROWNED. FROM 1929 TO 1973, DON BURNAP RAN THE MAILBOAT. TODAY, THE "PRESIDENT HARRISON" STILL CARRIES MAIL TO SOME 85 PATRONS AND ALSO GIVES TOURS.

THE PRESIDENT HARRISON

US MAIL

35 FOOT DIESEL

PICKLE BOAT

THE "PICKLE BOAT," A FLOATING GROCERY STORE, WAS A FAMILIAR SIGHT ON THE FIRST 4 LAKES IN THE FULTON CHAIN FROM 1905 TO 1940. MARKS AND WILCOX, A GROCERY AND FUEL SUPPLY STORE IN OLD FORGE, STARTED IT BECAUSE OF ISOLATED CAMPS AN HOTELS. THE STEAMBOAT'S REAL NAME WAS "THE MOHAWK," BUT IT GOT NICK — NAMED BECAUSE OF A LARGE PICKLE BARREL ON THE REAR DECK. IT TRAVELED FROM OLD FORGE TO INLET WITH OWNER/BUTCHER CHARLIE WILCOX, A PILOT, A FIREMAN, CLERKS FILLING ORDERS AND BOYS DELIVERING. THE BOAT HAD FRESH MEAT, MILK, VEGETABLES, FRUITS AND KEROSENE. ON MON/WED/FRI/SAT THE BOAT LEFT AT 7 AM FOR INLET AND RETURNED AT 6 PM BUT ON TUE/THUR THE BOAT STAYED OVERNIGHT IN INLET AND PICKED UP ICE AND SUPPLIES FROM OLD FORGE FOR THE RETURN TRIP. THE "PICKLE BOAT" ENDED SERVICE BECAUSE ROADS IMPROVED AND CHARLIE WILCOX WAS GETTING TOO OLD FOR A LONG WORKWEEK.

NORTON "BUSTER" BIRD JR.

NORTON "BUSTER" OR "BUS" BIRD JR. (1908-2000), AN ADIRONDACK BUSH PILOT FOR 44 YEARS, SKILLED WOODSMAN, GUIDE, AND CAPTAIN OF HIS 100-PASSENGER OSPREY GIVING SCENIC CRUISES DURING THE 1950S, GREW UP IN RAQUETTE LAKE. BUS STARTED A SEAPLANE SERVICE IN 1948 AND CARRIED HUNTERS AND FISHERMEN TO WILDERNESS CAMPS. HE ALSO WORKED FOR THE DEC, FLYING SEARCH AND RESCUE MISSIONS AND FIRE-SPOTTING. ONE YEAR HE TURNED IN 29 SMOKES TO THE RANGERS. BUS ALSO PILOTED BIOLOGISTS STUDYING BIG GAME AND MARINE LIFE. HE HAD A FEW CLOSE CALLS DUE TO ENGINE FAILURE AND POOR WEATHER. ONCE, FLYING HOME FROM UTICA, HIS ENGINE DIED. HE GLIDED TILL HE SAW THE BLACK RIVER. WHILE LANDING HE NARROWLY MISSED POWER LINES AND A 15' SAND BANK. A FARMER DROVE UP AND ASKED: "WHY DID YOU LAND IN A RIVER FULL OF STUMPS?" BUS BOUGHT 10 GALLONS OF GAS FROM THE FARMER AND GOT HOME SAFELY.

©2006 MAITLY PODSKOCH ~ SAM GLANZMAN

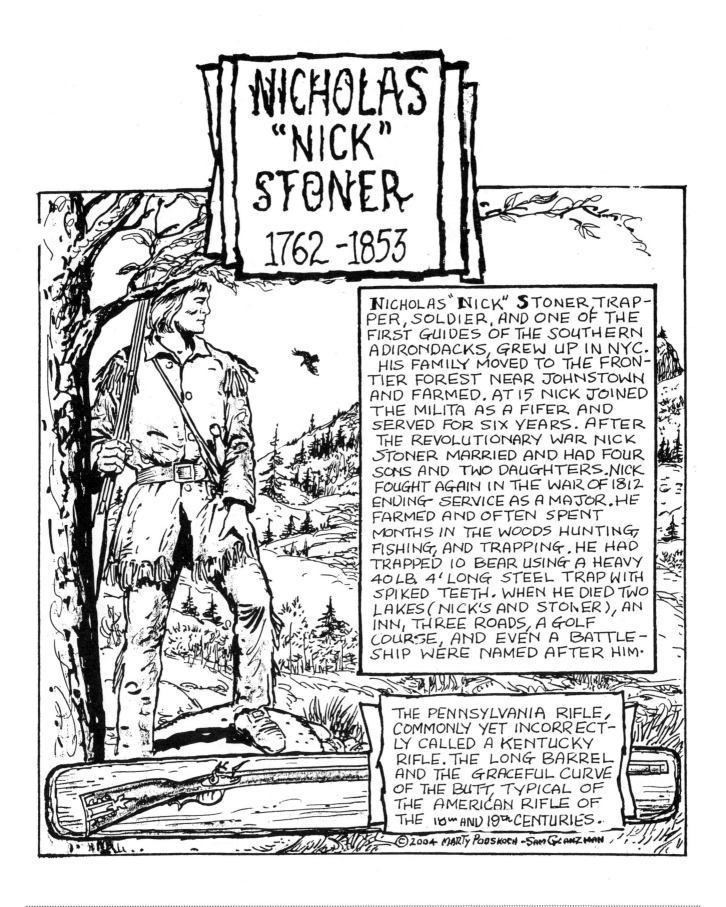

NICHOLAS "NICK" STONER
1762-1853

NICHOLAS "NICK" STONER, TRAP-PER, SOLDIER, AND ONE OF THE FIRST GUIDES OF THE SOUTHERN ADIRONDACKS, GREW UP IN NYC. HIS FAMILY MOVED TO THE FRON-TIER FOREST NEAR JOHNSTOWN AND FARMED. AT 15 NICK JOINED THE MILITA AS A FIFER AND SERVED FOR SIX YEARS. AFTER THE REVOLUTIONARY WAR NICK STONER MARRIED AND HAD FOUR SONS AND TWO DAUGHTERS. NICK FOUGHT AGAIN IN THE WAR OF 1812 ENDING SERVICE AS A MAJOR. HE FARMED AND OFTEN SPENT MONTHS IN THE WOODS HUNTING, FISHING, AND TRAPPING. HE HAD TRAPPED 10 BEAR USING A HEAVY 40 LB. 4' LONG STEEL TRAP WITH SPIKED TEETH. WHEN HE DIED TWO LAKES (NICK'S AND STONER), AN INN, THREE ROADS, A GOLF COURSE, AND EVEN A BATTLE-SHIP WERE NAMED AFTER HIM.

THE PENNSYLVANIA RIFLE, COMMONLY YET INCORRECT-LY CALLED A KENTUCKY RIFLE. THE LONG BARREL AND THE GRACEFUL CURVE OF THE BUTT, TYPICAL OF THE AMERICAN RIFLE OF THE 18TH AND 19TH CENTURIES.

©2004 MARTY PODSKOCH - SAM GLANZMAN

THOMAS MEACHAM 1770-1849

THOMAS MEACHAM, KNOWN THROUGHOUT THE ADIRONDACKS AS DOCTOR MEACHAM FOR HIS KNOWLEDGE OF HERBS, WAS ONE OF THE GREATEST HUNTERS IN FRANKLIN COUNTY. HE LIVED IN A LOG CABIN ON NORTHWEST BAY ROAD ON THE ST. REGIS RIVER NEAR NICHOLVILLE. MEACHAM KEPT AN ACCOUNT OF THE ANIMALS HE KILLED: WOLVES 214, PANTHERS 77, BEARS 210, AND DEER 2,550. HIS TRAPS WERE ALWAYS OUT, AND ONE DAY IN EXAMINING THEM HE FOUND TWO WOLVES AND A BEAR AND SHOT ANOTHER BEAR ON THE WAY. HIS BOUNTY FOR THESE WAS $185. DOC RANGED FAR AND WIDE THROUGH FIELDS AND FOREST FOR HEALING PLANTS AND WHIPPED UP CURES FOR THE AILMENTS OF THE LOCAL FOLK. MEACHAM LAKE, NORTH OF PAUL SMITHS, AND A HOTEL ON ITS SHORES WERE NAMED AFTER THOMAS MEACHAM.

© 2005 MARTY PODSKOCH – SAM GLANZMAN

ADIRONDACK PANTHER

THE ADIRONDACK PANTHER (AKA MOUNTAIN LION, PUMA AND COUGAR) WAS HUNTED TO NEAR EXTINCTION BY THE TURN OF THE 20TH CENTURY. IN 1871 ITS HABIT OF KILLING FARMERS LIVESTOCK AND THREATENING PEOPLE LED TO A STATE BOUNTY OF $20 FOR A PANTHER'S HIDE AND SKULL.

THE PANTHER WAS KNOWN TO FOLLOW PEOPLE AND LEAP ON THEM FROM TREES AND CLIFFS. A PANTHER'S SCREECH WAS A TERRIFYING SOUND. GEORGE MUIR, A BOUNTY HUNTER FROM HARRISVILLE, KILLED 67 PANTHERS BY 1890. IN 1903 THE MALONE FARMER REPORTED CHARLES LAKE OF HARRISVILLE WAS CHASED BY A PANTHER WHILE CAMPING. HE WAS ABLE TO CLIMB A TREE, MAKE A TORCH, AND THEN USE IT AS A SHIELD AS HE RAN BACK INTO CAMP. THE FRUSTRATED PANTHER'S CRIES RANG THROUGH THE WOODS.
   TODAY, ONCE AGAIN, THERE ARE STORIES OF SIGHTINGS OF THE ADIRONDACK PANTHER.

© 2006 MARTY PODSKOCH - SAM GLANZMAN

JOHN CHENEY

1800-1877

JOHN CHENEY, A LEGENDARY GUIDE AND HUNTER, CAME FROM TICONDEROGA TO NEWCOMB IN 1830 WITH ONLY HIS KNAPSACK, GUN, AND DOG. DURING THE NEXT 13 YEARS HE CLAIMED HE KILL-ED 600 DEER, 400 MARTEN, 19 MOOSE, 48 BEARS, 30 OTTER 7 WILD CATS AND 6 WOLVES, 1 PANTHER AND THE LAST BEAVER IN N.Y. ONCE HE BROKE HIS RIFLE HITTING A WOLF OVER ITS HEAD. AFTERWARD, HE HUNTED WITH AN 11" PISTOL. ONE DAY HE SLIPPED SNOWSHOEING AND FELL INTO A LARGE BEAR'S DEN. CHENEY WAS LOSING THE BATTLE WITH THE BEAR WHEN HIS DOG DREW THE BEAR AWAY. AN-OTHER STORY TOLD OF A PANTHER LEAPING AT CHENEY WHO SHOT THE CAT IN THE BRAIN. IN AUGUST 1837 CHENEY GUIDED GEOLOGIST EBENEZER EMMONS FOR THE FIRST RECORDED ASCENT OF MT. MARCY. CHENEY REMARKED ABOUT THE VIEW "IT MAKES A MAN FEEL WHAT IT IS TO HAVE ALL CREATION UNDER HIS FEET."

SNAKE EYE
ALVAH DUNNING

1816 – 1910

ALVAH "SNAKE EYE" DUNNING, THE HERMIT GUIDE OF RAQUETTE LAKE, LEARNED HIS CRAFT AT THE AGE OF SIX FROM HIS FATHER, A RUTHLESS INDIAN FIGHTER. ALVAH BOASTED KILLING HIS FIRST MOOSE WHEN HE WAS ELEVEN AND BEGAN GUIDING AT THE AGE OF 12. SNAKE EYE (SO CALLED BY INDIANS FOR HIS SMALL, SHARP EYES) WAS ABLE TO LURE ANIMALS TO HIM BY MIMICKING THEM. DUNNING'S WOODSMAN'S SKILL DREW MANY SPORTSMEN, INCLUDING THE FUTURE PRESIDENT GROVER CLEVELAND, BUT HE DID NOT LIKE THEM: "I'D RUTHER THEY'D STAY TER HUM AND KEEP THEIR MONEY." ALTHOUGH HE LIVED MOST OF HIS LIFE ALONE IN THE WOODS, ALVAH DIED OF ASPHYXIATION AFTER BLOWING OUT A GAS HEATER PILOT LIGHT IN THE ROOM OF A UTICA HOTEL WHERE HE WAS STAYING.

© MARTY PODSKOCH - SAM GLANZMAN 2004

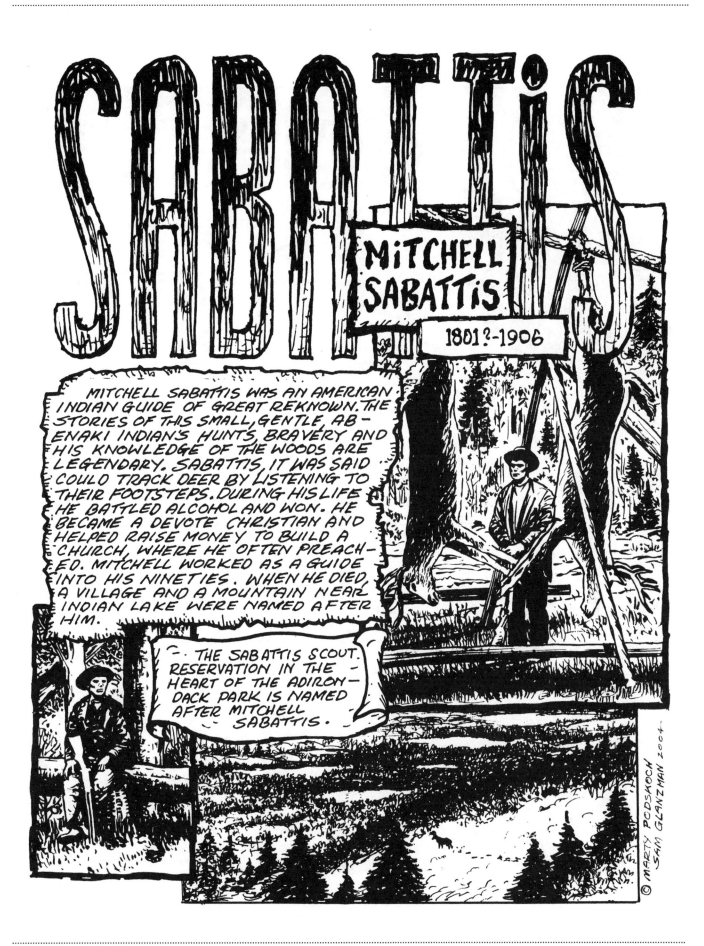

SABATTIS

MITCHELL SABATTIS

1801?-1906

MITCHELL SABATTIS WAS AN AMERICAN INDIAN GUIDE OF GREAT REKNOWN. THE STORIES OF THIS SMALL, GENTLE, ABENAKI INDIAN'S HUNTS, BRAVERY AND HIS KNOWLEDGE OF THE WOODS ARE LEGENDARY. SABATTIS, IT WAS SAID COULD TRACK DEER BY LISTENING TO THEIR FOOTSTEPS. DURING HIS LIFE HE BATTLED ALCOHOL AND WON. HE BECAME A DEVOTE CHRISTIAN AND HELPED RAISE MONEY TO BUILD A CHURCH, WHERE HE OFTEN PREACHED. MITCHELL WORKED AS A GUIDE INTO HIS NINETIES. WHEN HE DIED, A VILLAGE AND A MOUNTAIN NEAR INDIAN LAKE WERE NAMED AFTER HIM.

THE SABATTIS SCOUT RESERVATION IN THE HEART OF THE ADIRONDACK PARK IS NAMED AFTER MITCHELL SABATTIS.

© MARTY PODSKOCH
SAM GLANZMAN 2004

GEORGE NESSMUK SEARS

1821-1890

George Washington Sears

GEORGE WASHINGTON SEARS GREW UP IN MASSACHUSETTS WHERE A YOUNG NARRAGANSETT INDIAN NAMED NESSMUK TAUGHT HIM HUNTING, FISHING AND CAMPING SKILLS. GEORGE WANDERED OUT WEST BECOMING A TEACHER, COWBOY, EDITOR, AND SILVER MINER AND LATER LIVED IN PENNSYLVANIA. IN 1880 GEORGE, UNDER THE PEN NAME "NESSMUK", WROTE LETTERS TO FOREST AND STREAM MAGAZINE. IN 1883 HE WROTE *WOODCRAFT, THE FIRST AMERICAN BOOK ON OUTDOOR LIFE. LATER, WEAK FROM TUBERCULOSIS, HE MADE THREE CANOE TRIPS IN THE ADIRONDACKS TO IMPROVE HIS HEALTH. J. HENRY RUSHTON BUILT AN ULTRA-LIGHT CANOE (9 LBS) FOR THE 5' TALL 105-POUND WRITER. * GEORGE AIMED TO HELP "OUTERS" "SMOOTH IT" INSTEAD OF "ROUGH IT" IN THE WOODS.

© MARTY PODSKOCH - SAM GLANZMAN 2005

ADIRONDACK GUIDEBOAT

THE ADIRONDACK GUIDE-BOAT, A SLEEK, SWIFT, LIGHT, WOODEN BOAT WITH POINTED ENDS AND OARS, WERE FIRST MADE BY GUIDES IN THE LONG LAKE AREA ABOUT 1840 WHEN SPORTSMEN BEGAN COMING TO THE ADIRONDACKS FOR HUNTING AND FISHING. THEY USED CEDER, SPRUCE, PINE, CHERRY OR ASH FOR THE FRAME. BEVELED SID-ING WAS OVERLAPPED AND FAS-TENED TO THE RIBS WITH ABOUT 4,000 SMALL COPPER, BRASS, OR BRONZE SCREWS AND 7,000 TACKS. THE RIBS WERE SHAPED FROM STRONG SPRUCE TREE ROOTS AND ATTACHED TO A BOT-TOM BOARD. THE CRAFT WAS 15-17' LONG AND ABLE TO CAR-RY TWO PEOPLE, THEIR GEAR, THEIR DOGS AND ANY GAME.
   GUIDES CARRIED THE 65-75 POUND BOAT ON THEIR SHOUL-DERS FROM LAKE TO LAKE. WILLIAM A. MARTIN, A GUIDEBOAT BUILDER IN SARANAC LAKE, DESIGNED A BOAT THAT WAS EVEN LIGHTER. AT FIRST PEOPLE LAUGHED AND CALLED IT, WILLIE ALLEN'S "EGG-SHELLS" BUT IT BECAME POPULAR JUST BECAUSE OF ITS LIGHTNESS.

NAT FOSTER

1766 ~ 1840

MART PODSKOCH ~ SAM GLANZMAN
©2005

NAT FOSTER, HUNTER & TRAPPER NEAR SALISBURY, EARNED $1,000 ONE SEASON SHOOTING 35 BEAR, 76 DEER, 25 WOLVES, AND TRAPPING NUMEROUS BEAVER, MINK, & MARTEN. USING A "DOUBLE SHOOTER" RIFLE AND HOLDING 6 LEAD BALLS BETWEEN HIS FINGERS NAT COULD SHOOT SIX HOLES IN A CIRCLE IN 60 SECONDS AT 200 FEET. HE WAS AN HONEST, FRIENDLY, AND GENEROUS MAN, BUT WAS SUSPICIOUS OF INDIANS AFTER SOME ABDUCTED HIS SISTER. NAT ELIMINATED DISHONEST INDIANS IN THE WOODS. WHEN HE MOVED TO FULTON CHAIN OF LAKES AN ENVIOUS INDIAN TRAPPER, PETER "DRID" WATERS THREATENED TO KILL NAT. ON SEPTEMBER 17, 1833 DRID ATTACKED NAT WITH A KNIFE AND LATER THAT DAY NAT RETALIATED BY SHOOTING DRID AT "INDIAN POINT" AT THE FOOT OF FIRST LAKE. NAT WAS TRIED FOR MURDER IN HERKIMER BUT WAS FOUND NOT GUILTY.

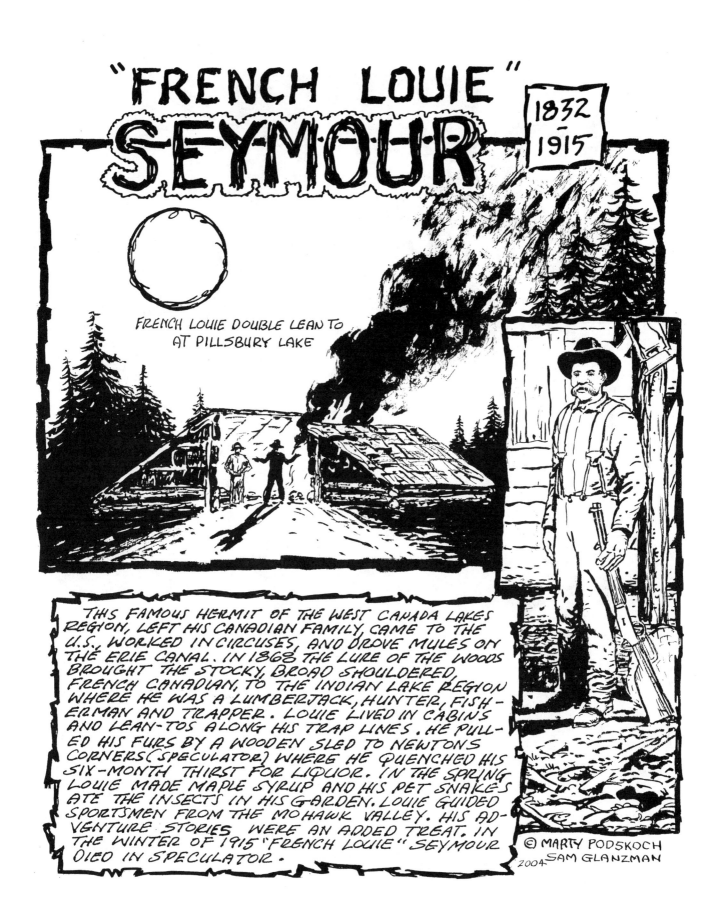

"FRENCH LOUIE" SEYMOUR

1832 – 1915

FRENCH LOUIE DOUBLE LEAN TO AT PILLSBURY LAKE

THIS FAMOUS HERMIT OF THE WEST CANADA LAKES REGION, LEFT HIS CANADIAN FAMILY, CAME TO THE U.S., WORKED IN CIRCUSES, AND DROVE MULES ON THE ERIE CANAL. IN 1868 THE LURE OF THE WOODS BROUGHT THE STOCKY, BROAD SHOULDERED, FRENCH CANADIAN, TO THE INDIAN LAKE REGION WHERE HE WAS A LUMBERJACK, HUNTER, FISH-ERMAN AND TRAPPER. LOUIE LIVED IN CABINS AND LEAN-TOS ALONG HIS TRAP LINES. HE PULL-ED HIS FURS BY A WOODEN SLED TO NEWTONS CORNERS (SPECULATOR) WHERE HE QUENCHED HIS SIX-MONTH THIRST FOR LIQUOR. IN THE SPRING LOUIE MADE MAPLE SYRUP AND HIS PET SNAKES ATE THE INSECTS IN HIS GARDEN. LOUIE GUIDED SPORTSMEN FROM THE MOHAWK VALLEY. HIS AD-VENTURE STORIES WERE AN ADDED TREAT. IN THE WINTER OF 1915 "FRENCH LOUIE" SEYMOUR DIED IN SPECULATOR.

© MARTY PODSKOCH
2004 SAM GLANZMAN

DEER JACKING, HUNTING DEER AT NIGHT WITH A LIGHT, WAS A COMMON PRACTICE IN THE ADIRONDACKS DURING THE 1800s. NATURE WRITER JOHN BURROUGHS WROTE ABOUT DEER JACKING IN HIS BOOK, WAKE ROBIN. A GUIDE TOOK HIM HUNTING ON A LAKE AT NIGHT. HE SAT IN THE BOW WITH A RIFLE. THE JACKLIGHT, A PORTABLE LANTERN HOLDING 3 CANDLES, WAS ON A 3' STAFF HELD BY A BAR NEXT TO HIM. HIS GUIDE IN THE STERN ROWED QUIETLY TILL HE HEARD A DEER ALONG THE SHORE. HE WHISPERED TO LIGHT THE CANDLES. IT TOOK THE NERVOUS BURROUGHS 4 MATCHES BUT HE FINALLY LIT THEM. HE SAW "TWO LUMINOUS SPOTS," AND THEN THE WHOLE DEER "TRANSFIXED" BY THE LIGHT. BURROUGHS' SHOT ECHOED OVER THE LAKE AND THE DEER RAN INTO THE WOODS. CARRYING THE JACK-LIGHT, BURROUGHS AND HIS GUIDE FOUND THE DEAD DEER CLOSE BY. DEER JACKING CONTINUED UNTIL 1897 WHEN N.Y. OUTLAW-ED THE PRACTICE BECAUSE IT WAS UNSPORTSMANLIKE.

© 2006 – MARTY PODSKOCH – SAM GLANZMAN

Julia Burton Preston
1898~1969

JULIA BURTON PRESTON, ONE OF THE FIRST LICENSED FEMALE GUIDES IN NYS, GREW UP IN A LOG CABIN IN PISECO LAKE. HER CANADIAN-INDIAN FATHER TAUGHT HER TO HUNT. AT 16 SHE MARRIED CHARLIE PRESTON AND THEY HUNTED, FISHED, AND TRAPPED TOGETHER. THEY LOVED ANIMALS AND RAISED A 3-LEGGED FOX, A MINK, AND RACCOONS AND BEAR CUBS. SHE GUIDED HUNTERS FOR $10 A DAY IN 1914. THE 4'10" GUIDE WAS A CRACK SHOT WITH HER WINCHESTER 25.20. ONCE SHE FOUND A LOST HUNTER BUT HAD A HARD TIME CONVINCING HIM TO FOLLOW HER. IF SHE SAW LIGHTNING THAT MIGHT CAUSE A FIRE ON HER TELEPHONE LINE, JULIA WOULD CUT IT WITH ONE SHOT. WHEN SHE DROVE A SCHOOL BUS SHE KEPT A RIFLE UNDER HER SEAT IN CASE SHE SAW GAME. ONE OF HER THREE CHILDREN, HOMER, BECAME A GAME PROTECTOR. HIS SUPERIORS SAID HE WAS THE BEST THEY EVER TRAINED. JULIA REPLIED, "HE SHOULD BE, I TAUGHT HIM EVERYTHING I KNOW ABOUT VIOLATING!" © MARTY PODSKOCH
2006 SAM GLANZMAN

NEHASANE PARK

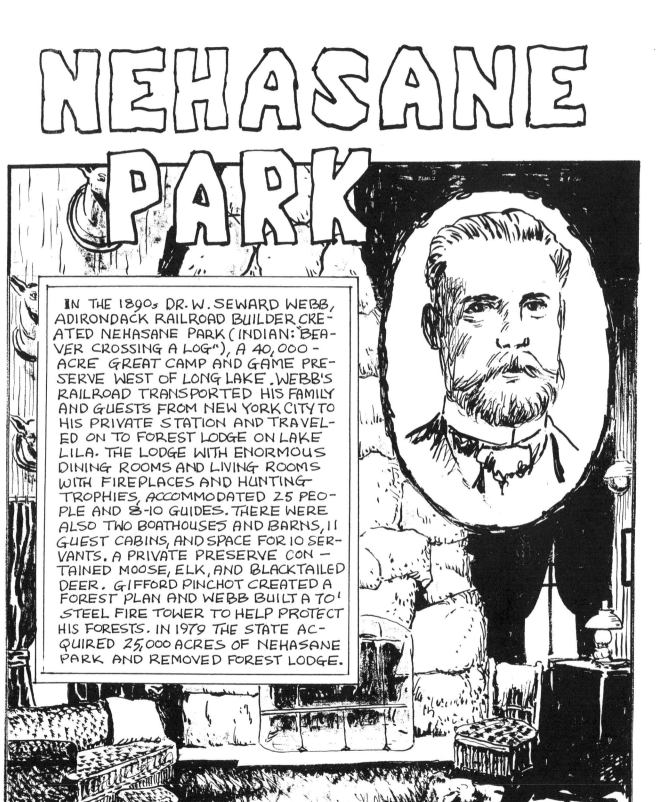

IN THE 1890s DR. W. SEWARD WEBB,
ADIRONDACK RAILROAD BUILDER CRE-
ATED NEHASANE PARK (INDIAN: "BEA-
VER CROSSING A LOG"), A 40,000-
ACRE GREAT CAMP AND GAME PRE-
SERVE WEST OF LONG LAKE. WEBB'S
RAILROAD TRANSPORTED HIS FAMILY
AND GUESTS FROM NEW YORK CITY TO
HIS PRIVATE STATION AND TRAVEL-
ED ON TO FOREST LODGE ON LAKE
LILA. THE LODGE WITH ENORMOUS
DINING ROOMS AND LIVING ROOMS
WITH FIREPLACES AND HUNTING
TROPHIES, ACCOMMODATED 25 PEO-
PLE AND 8-10 GUIDES. THERE WERE
ALSO TWO BOATHOUSES AND BARNS, 11
GUEST CABINS, AND SPACE FOR 10 SER-
VANTS. A PRIVATE PRESERVE CON-
TAINED MOOSE, ELK, AND BLACKTAILED
DEER. GIFFORD PINCHOT CREATED A
FOREST PLAN AND WEBB BUILT A 70'
STEEL FIRE TOWER TO HELP PROTECT
HIS FORESTS. IN 1979 THE STATE AC-
QUIRED 25,000 ACRES OF NEHASANE
PARK AND REMOVED FOREST LODGE.

©MARTY
PODSKOCH '04

GREAT CAMP PINE KNOT

WILLIAM WEST DURANT

THE ADIRONDACK STYLE OF ARCHITECTURE, ALSO KNOWN AS 'GREAT CAMPS,' ORIGINATED AT CAMP PINE KNOT AT RAQUETTE LAKE IN 1879. 'CAMP PINE KNOT' GOT ITS NAME FROM A 3-FOOT WOODEN KNOT USED IN ITS CONSTRUCTION.

WILLIAM WEST DURANT, ARCHTECT AND ENTREPRENEUR, GUIDED HUNDREDS OF LOCAL ARTISANS IN USING MATERIALS FROM THE LAND TO BUILD LOG STRUCTURES SIMILAR TO SWISS CHALETS, MASONS USED NATIVE STONE FOR FOUNDATIONS AND FIREPLACES. CARPENTERS USED ROOTS, TWIGS, AND SMALL LIMBS TO MAKE FURNITURE. BARK WAS USED AS WALLPAPER.

THE CAMP'S 'SWISS COTTAGE' WAS TWO STORIES TALL WITH A LARGE LIVING ROOM AND FOUR BEDROOMS. SEPARATE RESIDENCES HAD KITCHENS, DINING AREAS, AND BEDROOMS CONNECTED BY COVERED WALKWAYS. IN 1895 DURANT SOLD THE 26-BUILDING CAMP TO RAILROAD EXECUTIVE COLLIS HUNTINGTON. DURANT BUILT SEVERAL OTHER RUSTIC ESTATES: UNCAS IN 1895 AND SAGAMORE IN 1900. DURANT'S ECO-FRIENDLY ADIRONDACK STYLE SPREAD THROUGHOUT THE U.S. AND BEYOND.

© 2006 - MARTY PODSKOCH - SAM GLANZMAN

CAMP SAGAMORE, BUILT IN 1897 ON 1,526 WILDERNESS-ACRES 4-MILES SOUTH OF RAQUETTE LAKE, WAS THE CREATION OF ARCHITECT WILLIAM WEST DURANT. THE MAIN BUILDING WAS A THREE-STORY CHALET WITH GAS LIGHTING, CENTRAL HEATING, BATHS WITH HOT WATER AND FLUSH TOILETS. THERE WERE ABOUT 60 OTHER BUILDINGS INCLUDING A DINING ROOM, KITCHEN, ROOT CELLAR, LAUNDRY, ICE HOUSE, BLACKSMITH SHOP, AND SCHOOLHOUSE. THE WIGWAM WAS A LODGE WHERE MEN COULD SMOKE CIGARS, DRINK, AND PLAY POKER. IT WAS SELF-SUFFICIENT WITH VEGETABLE GARDENS AND FARM ANIMALS. IN 1901 DURANT SOLD SAGAMORE TO ALFRED G. VANDERBILT, WHO WENT DOWN WITH THE LUSITANIA IN 1915. HIS WIDOW, MARGARET EMERSON, ENTERTAINED HER FAMILY AND HIGH-SOCIETY FRIENDS DURING THE SUMMER AND THE CHRISTMAS HOLIDAY. GUESTS ENJOYED LAVISH DINNERS SERVED BY SERVENTS FROM BRITAIN. THERE WAS BOWLING, TENNIS, HORSEBACK RIDING, CROQUET, HUNTING, SWIMMING, FISHING AND BOATING. TODAY CAMP SAGAMORE IS OWNED BY THE NONPROFIT SAGAMORE INSTITUTE OF THE ADIRONDACKS. CAMP SAGAMORE IS OPEN FOR GUIDED TOURS AND LODGING.

© 2006 - MARTY PODSKOCH - SAM GLANZMAN

CAMP SANTANONI, AN OUTSTANDING EXAMPLE OF LATE 19TH-CENTURY ADIRONDACK RUSTIC ARCHITECTURE IN THE "GREAT CAMP" STYLE. IT WAS STARTED IN 1892 FOR ROBERT C. PRUYN (1847-1934), A PROMINENT ALBANY BANKER. THE CAMP EVENTUALLY INCLUDED NEARLY 4 DOZEN BUILDINGS IN 3 COMPLEXES SPREAD ACROSS 12,900 ACRES. AT THE ENTRANCE, NEAR NEWCOMB, THERE WAS AN ENORMOUS STONE ARCHED GATEHOUSE AND SEVERAL OTHER BUILDINGS. A MILE IN WAS THE FARM COMPLEX WITH HUGE BARNS, A STONE CREAMERY, SMOKE HOUSE, AND 4 FARM HOUSES WHERE THEY PRODUCED ENOUGH MEAT AND PRODUCE FOR THE WHOLE CAMP. THE MAIN LODGE ON NEWCOMB LAKE WAS INSPIRED BY TRADITIONAL JAPANESE ARCHITECTURE. IT CONSISTS OF 6 LOG BUILDINGS UNITED BY A COMMON 15,000 SQUARE FOOT ROOF. GUESTS HAD A SPECTACULAR VIEW OF SANTANONI MT. (ABENAKI INDIAN PRONUNCIATION OF SAINT ANTHONY) AND OTHER HIGH PEAKS. IT IS CURRENTLY BEING RESTORED, BY NEW YORK STATE AND ITS PARTNERS, ADIRONDACK ARCHITECTURAL HERITAGE AND THE TOWN OF NEWCOMB.

© 2006 - MARTY PODSKOCH - SAM GLANZMAN

LITCHFIELD PARK, ONE OF THE MOST UNUSUAL CAMPS IN THE ADIRONDACKS, WAS ESTABLISHED BY EDWARD LITCHFIELD, A RETIRED LAWYER, IN 1893 WHEN HE PURCHASED ABOUT 9,000 ACRES SOUTH OF TUPPER LAKE IN FRANKLIN CO. HE CAME TO THE ADIRONDACKS IN 1866 TO HUNT AND FISH BUT AFTER 10 YEARS THE WOLVES AND PANTHERS DISAPPEARED AND IT DIDN'T SEEM WILD TO HIM ANYMORE SO HE HUNTED IN THE ROCKY MTS., ASIA, AND AFRICA. HE CAME BACK TO THE ADIRONDACKS AND CREATED THE PARK TO BREED WILD GAME. AN 8' HIGH WIRE FENCE SURROUNDED THE LAND FOR HIS IMPORT-ED BEAVER, MOOSE, ELK, DEER, BEAR, HARE, PHEASANT, AND OTHER BIRDS. HIS EFFORTS FAILED WHEN ANIMALS DIED, ESCAPED THROUGH DAMAGED FENCES, OR WERE KILLED BY POACHERS. LITCHFIELD ALSO BUILT A THREE-STORY, FRENCH CHATEAU OF STONE AND CONCRETE AND DECORATED IT WITH ANIMAL HEADS AND AN ART GALLERY. THE PARK IS STILL OWNED BY THE LITCHFIELD FAMILY, WHICH MANAGES THE FOREST FOR WOOD PRODUCTS.

© 2006 MARTY PODSKOCH - SAM GLANZMAN

BRANDRETH PARK

BRANDRETH LAKE

WOMEN PACKING
PILLS AT
THE FACTORY
CA. 1900

BRANDRETH PARK IS ONE OF THE FIRST PRIVATE WILDERNESS PRESERVES IN THE ADIRONDACKS. IT IS NAMED AFTER DR. BENJAMIN BRANDRETH WHO WAS BORN IN LEEDS, ENGLAND AND CAME TO THE U.S. IN 1835 WITH A FORMULA FOR VEGETABLE LAXATIVE PILLS. HE PRO-DUCED THE PILLS IN A FACTORY IN OSSINING, NY AND AMASSED A LARGE FORTUNE. BRANDRETH BECAME A NYS SENATOR AND PUR-CHASED TOWNSHIP 39 IN THE NORTHWEST CORNER OF HAMILTON COUNTY IN 1851. HIS SONS FRANKLIN AND RALPH, AND SON-IN-LAW EDWIN McALPIN MANAGED THE ESTATE AND EACH BUILT CAMPS FOR OUTDOOR SPORTS ON THE NORTH END OF BRANDRETH LAKE. THEY USED THE MOHAWK MALONE RAILROAD (1892) TO ACCESS THE PARK AND TO TRANSPORT LUMBER (1912-1920) LOGGED BY THE MAC-A-MAC LUMBER COMPANY. A MODEST VILLAGE GREW AT THE BRANDRETH STATION BUT WAS ABANDONED AFTER 1962 WHEN TRAIN SERVICE ENDED. TODAY DESCENDANTS OF DR. BRANDRETH MANAGE TO PRE-SERVE ITS WILD CHARACTER.

© 2006 - MARTY PODSKOCH - SAM GLANZMAN

ROCKEFELLER LAMORA DISPUTE

WILLIAM ROCKEFELLER, CO-FOUNDER OF STANDARD OIL WITH HIS OLDER BROTHER JOHN D., SURPRISED SEVERAL HUNDRED RESIDENTS OF BRANDON (6 M. WEST OF PAUL SMITHS), WHEN HE BOUGHT ALL THE LAND AROUND THEM DURING THE SUMMER OF 1898 AND CLAIMED TO OWN A ROAD LEADING TO TOWN. EVENTUALLY MOST SOLD THEIR LAND TO HIM EXCEPT OLIVER LAMORA AND THE PERYEAS FAMILY WHO NEVER SOLD. LAMORA CONTINUED TO HUNT AND FISH ON ROCKEFELLER'S PRESERVE. THE TALL GRAY-HAIRED GENTLEMAN WAS ARRESTED IN 1902. NEIGHBORS HELPED PAY LEGAL EXPENSES AND LAWYERS VOLUNTEERED TO DEFEND HIM. OLIVER ARGUED THE STATE STOCKED ROCKEFELLER'S PONDS, SO HE HAD THE RIGHT TO FISH THERE. HE BECAME A NATIONAL HERO FOR STANDING UP TO THE ROBBER BARON. FINALLY, LAMORA LOST AN APPEAL AND HAD TO PAY 18 CENTS IN DAMAGES AND COULD NO LONGER FISH ON ROCKEFELLER'S PRESERVE. ROCKEFELLER FINALLY GOT THE LAND IN 1915 FROM LAMORA'S SON AND HEIR.

© 2007 - MARTY PODSKOCH ~ SAM GLANZMAN

"THE LAST OF THE MOHICANS" BY JAMES FENIMORE COOPER (1789-1851), IS ONE OF HIS LEATHERSTOCK— ING TALES. IT IS SET DURING THE FRENCH AND INDIAN WAR IN 1757. BRITISH MAJOR DUNCAN IS BRINGING ALICE AND CORA TO COLONEL MUNRO, THEIR FATHER, AT FORT WILLIAM HENRY ON LAKE GEORGE, WHICH IS BESIEGED BY THE FRENCH. MAGUA, A VILLAINOUS HURON, LEADS THE GROUP ASTRAY AND ENCOUNTERS THE WOODSMAN NATTY BUMPPO ("HAWKEYE") AND TWO MOHICAN COM— PANIONS, CHINGACHGOOK AND UNCAS. MAGUA GATHERS INDIANS TO ATTACK THE GROUP HIDING IN CAVES NEAR GLENS FALLS. THE WOODSMEN ESCAPE AND SEEK HELP. MAGUA CAPTURES THE GROUP IN THE CAVE AND LATER PROPOSES TO CORA WHO REFUSES HIM. THE WOODSMEN SAVE THE CAPTIVES BUT MAGUA ESCAPES. THE GROUP REACHES FORT WIL— LIAM HENRY WHICH IS THEN CAPTURED BY THE FRENCH. THE INDIANS MASSACRE THE BRIT— ISH AND MAGUA ESCAPES WITH THE TWO SIS— TERS. THE WOODSMEN PURSUE HIM NORTH OF THE LAKE. FINALLY CORA, UNCAS AND MAGUA ARE KILLED LEAVING CHINGACHGOOK THE LAST MOHICAN.

COOPERS CAVE, GLEN FALLS, N.Y. MADE FAMOUS BY COOPERS "THE LAST OF THE MO— HICANS"

© 2005 MARTY PODSKOCH-SAM GLANZMAN

"ADIRONDACK" MURRAY

1840   1904

WILLIAM HENRY HARRISON "ADIRONDACK" MURRAY, A BOSTON MINISTER, WROTE "ADVENTURES IN THE WILDERNESS" (1869), A GUIDE BOOK THAT INSPIRED A FLOOD OF TOURISTS TO THE ADIRONDACK MOUNTAINS. MURRAY GAVE ADVICE ON HOW TO TRAVEL, WHERE TO STAY, AND WHICH GUIDES WERE MOST RELIABLE. TEN CHAPTERS RELATED TALES OF CATCHING HUGE FISH, HUNTING, AND BRAVING A CANOE TRIP OVER WATERFALLS WITH HIS GUIDE JOHN PLUMLY OF LONG LAKE. MURRAY'S READERS DEVOURED HIS STORIES AND LEFT THE CITIES FOR MURRAY'S PARADISE. "... TO HAVE A LAKE OF CRYSTAL WATER FOR YOUR WASH-BOWL, THE MORNING ZEPHYR FOR A TOWEL, THE WHITEST SAND FOR SOAP AND THE ODORS OF AROMATIC TREES FOR PERFUMES." MURRAY'S BOOK SPURRED THE DEVELOPMENT OF TOURISM IN THE ADIRONDACKS. © MARTY PODSKOCH-SAM GLANZMAN 2004

NED BUNTLINE·
1821   1886

EDWARD ZANE CARROLL JUDSON, "NED BUNTLINE" WROTE OVER 400 POPULAR ACTION AND HISTORICAL ROMANCE NOVELS ABOUT PIRATES, POLITICS, THE CIVIL WAR AND THE WILD WEST. NED HAD THE COLT FACTORY MAKE A .45 WITH A 12" BARREL. HE PRESENTED THIS "BUNTLINE SPECIAL" TO MARSHALS WYATT EARP AND BAT MASTERSON.
BUNTLINE ALSO POPULARIZED W.F. COOY, IN HIS PLAY, "BUFFALO BILL." DURING THE 1850's NED CAME TO THE ADIRONDACKS TO WRITE IN SOLITUDE AT HIS HOME, "EAGLE'S NEST" ON EAGLE LAKE (BELOW BLUE MT. LAKE). WHILE THERE HE ENJOYED HUNTING AND FISHING AND WROTE WILD LIFE STORIES. HE LEFT THE ADIRONDACKS AND FOUGHT IN THE CIVIL WAR. HE FINALLY SETTLED IN HIS BIRTHPLACE, STAMFORD, N.Y. IN THE CATSKILLS...

©MARTY PODSKOCH —SAM GLANZMAN 2004.

"PHILOSOPHER'S CAMP"

THE SATURDAY CLUB, A GATHERING OF INTEL-
LECTUAL GIANTS FROM CIVILIZED BOSTON, CAME
TO THE WILDERNESS AROUND FOLLANSBY POND
NEAR AMPERSAND MT. IN JULY 1858 TO LIVE A SIM-
PLE HEALTHY LIFE IN NATURE. ARTIST WILLIAM
JAMES STILLMAN, AN AVID WOODSMAN, PERSUADED
RALPH WALDO EMERSON, JAMES RUSSELL LOWELL,
LOUIS AGGASIZ (SCIENTIFIC NATURALIST), JOHN
HOLMES (BROTHER OF OLIVER WENDELL), ETC. TO
LEAVE SAFE BOSTON AND ROUGH IT. EIGHT AD-
IRONDACK GUIDES HELPED WITH THE CAMPING
GEAR, TARGET SHOOTING, HUNTING, FISHING, AND
HIKING. THE MEN LIVED IN A PRIMITIVE SPRUCE-
DARK SHELTER WITH AN OPEN FRONT FACING A
FIREPLACE. THEY SLEPT ON FIR BRANCHES. RALPH
W. EMERSON WROTE, "UP WITH THE DAWN, THEY
FANCIED THE LIGHT AIR/ THAT CIRCLED FRESHLY
IN THE FOREST DRESS/ MADE THEM BOYS AGAIN."
THE MEN FORMED THE ADIRONDACK CLUB, PUR-
CHASED LAND AND BUILT A PERMANENT CLUB-
HOUSE CALLED THE PHILOSOPHER'S CAMP.

© 2005 MARTY PODSKOCH SAM GLANZMAN

JOHN BURROUGHS, TEACHER, NATURALIST, WRITER AND POET, WROTE AT HIS FAMILY FARMHOUSE, "WOODCHUCK LODGE" IN THE CATSKILLS, AND "RIVER-BY" AND "SLABSIDES" NEAR THE HUDSON RIVER. WALT WHITMAN, JOHN MUIR, ANDREW CARNEGIE, HENRY FORD, THOMAS EDISON AND TEDDY ROOSEVELT WERE HIS FRIENDS. IN HIS 28 BOOKS BURROUGHS TAUGHT COUNTLESS AMERICANS TO APPRECIATE NATURE.

"EACH OF YOU HAS THE WHOLE WEALTH OF THE UNIVERSE AT YOUR VERY DOOR"

JOHN DESCRIBES HIS AUGUST 1863 TRIP THROUGH THE ADIRONDACKS IN "WAKE-ROBIN." HE AND A FRIEND WERE GUIDED TO THE BOREAS RIVER, LAKE SANFORD, AND THE LOWER AND UPPER WORKS OF THE McINTYRE MINE NEAR NEWCOMB WHERE THEY SAW THE MAGNIFICENT HIGH PEAKS, EXPLORED, HUNTED, AND FISHED. BURROUGHS' WRITINGS AFFECTED HIS FRIEND, TEDDY ROOSEVELT, AND LED TO HIS CONSERVATION EFFORTS IN THE ADIRONDACKS AND NATIONWIDE WHEN HE WAS GOVERNOR OF NY AND PRESIDENT.

© MARTY PODSKOCH
SAM GLANZMAN 2005

ANNE LaBASTILLE

ANNE LaBASTILLE, INTERNATIONALLY RENOWNED CONSERVATIONIST WITH A Ph.D. IN WILDLIFE ECOLOGY, ADIRONDACK GUIDE, PHOTOGRAPHER AND AUTHOR OF 160 ARTICLES AND 10 BOOKS. HER WOODSWOMAN SERIES SPANS 3 DECADES OF HER LIVING IN A CABIN IN THE DEEP WOODS OF THE ADIRONDACKS WITHOUT ELECTRICITY, TELEPHONE OR INDOOR PLUMBING. ANNE CHOPPED WOOD FOR HER STOVE, BATHED IN THE LAKE, AND HAULED GROCERIES BY BOAT OR SLED IN THE WINTER. HER DO-IT-YOURSELF AND USE-IT-AGAIN ATTITUDE EMBODIES HER PHILOSOPHY AND PRACTICAL NATURE. "IT'S HOW WE MUST LIVE IN THE 21 ST CENTURY," SHE WRITES, "IF WE ARE TO HUSBAND OUR NATURAL RESOURCES AND SAVE WILDLIFE AND WILDLANDS." SHE WAS A COMMISSIONER OF THE ADIRONDACK PARK AGENCY AND FOUGHT TO PROTECT THE WILDERNESS. WHEN SHE IS NOT ON ASSIGNMENT THESE DAYS SHE LIVES IN HER FARMHOUSE NEAR WESTPORT OR HER CABIN ON BLACK BEAR LAKE.

© 2005 MARTY PODSKOCH - SAM GLANZMAN

WINSLOW HOMER 1836-1910

WINSLOW HOMER, ONE OF THE GREATEST AMERICAN PAINTERS, BEGAN VISITING THE BAKER'S FARM, A FORMER LOGGING CAMP IN THE ADIRONDACK WILDERNESS, NEAR MINERVA IN SOUTHERN ESSEX COUNTY IN 1870. HE WAS AN AVID FISHERMAN AND PAINTED SCENES OF FISHERMEN, GUIDES, LOGGERS AND TRAPPERS. RUFUS WALLACE AND MICHAEL FRANCIS FLYNN, TWO LOCAL GUIDES, POSED FOR MOST OF HIS PAINTINGS. THE BAKER FAMILY SOLD THE PROPERTY TO A CONSERVATION-MINDED GROUP THE NORTH WOODS CLUB. HOMER ALSO MADE A FEW VISITS TO KEENE VALLEY. HIS LAST VISIT TO MINERVA WAS JUST TWO MONTHS BEFORE HIS DEATH. HIS TWENTY-ONE VISITS OVER FORTY-YEARS RESULTED IN ABOUT 120 WATERCOLOR AND OIL PAINTINGS OF THE GREAT ADIRONDACK WILDERNESS.

© 2004

MARTY POUSKOCH
SAM GLANZMAN

FREDERIC REMINGTON

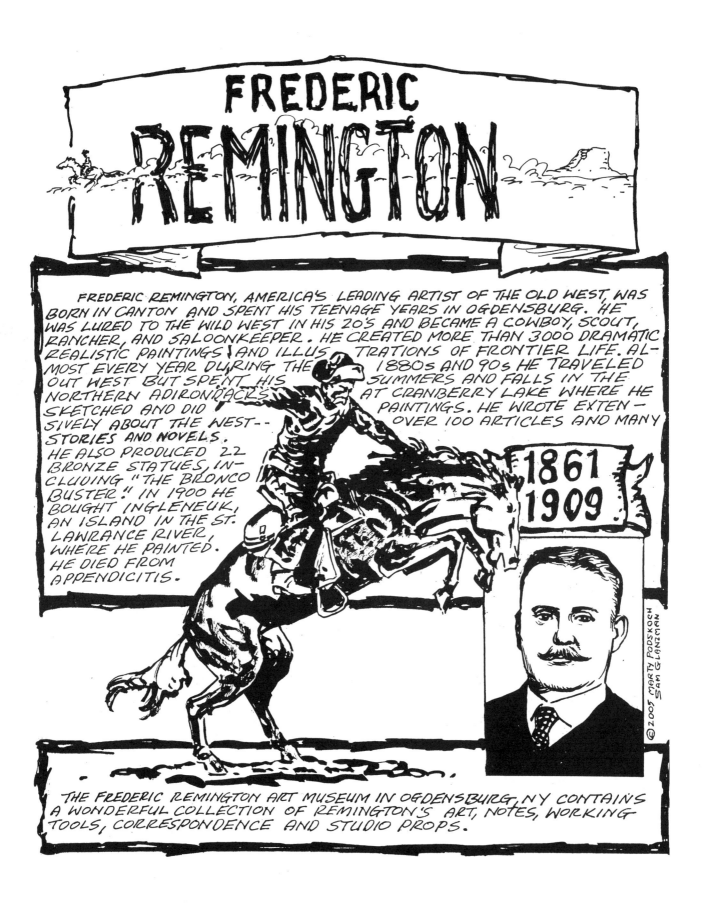

FREDERIC REMINGTON, AMERICA'S LEADING ARTIST OF THE OLD WEST, WAS BORN IN CANTON AND SPENT HIS TEENAGE YEARS IN OGDENSBURG. HE WAS LURED TO THE WILD WEST IN HIS 20'S AND BECAME A COWBOY, SCOUT, RANCHER, AND SALOONKEEPER. HE CREATED MORE THAN 3000 DRAMATIC REALISTIC PAINTINGS AND ILLUS- TRATIONS OF FRONTIER LIFE. AL- MOST EVERY YEAR DURING THE 1880s AND 90s HE TRAVELED OUT WEST BUT SPENT HIS SUMMERS AND FALLS IN THE NORTHERN ADIRONDACKS AT CRANBERRY LAKE WHERE HE SKETCHED AND DID PAINTINGS. HE WROTE EXTEN- SIVELY ABOUT THE WEST-- OVER 100 ARTICLES AND MANY STORIES AND NOVELS.
HE ALSO PRODUCED 22 BRONZE STATUES, IN- CLUDING "THE BRONCO BUSTER." IN 1900 HE BOUGHT INGLENEUK, AN ISLAND IN THE ST. LAWRANCE RIVER, WHERE HE PAINTED. HE DIED FROM APPENDICITIS.

1861
1909

© 2005 MARTY PODSKOCH
SAM GLANZMAN

THE FREDERIC REMINGTON ART MUSEUM IN OGDENSBURG, NY CONTAINS A WONDERFUL COLLECTION OF REMINGTON'S ART, NOTES, WORKING TOOLS, CORRESPONDENCE AND STUDIO PROPS.

GEORGIA O'KEEFFE

GEORGIA O'KEEFFE

1887
1986

OLD MAPLE, LAKE GEORGE
1926

GEORGIA O'KEEFFE WAS BORN NEAR SUN PRARIE WISCONSIN. IN 1905 SHE BEGAN STUDYING ART AT THE SCHOOL OF THE ART INSTITUTE OF CHIGAGO. - IN 1907, MOVING TO NEW YORK CITY, SHE ATTENDED THE ART STUDENTS LEAGUE. SHE WOULD MOVE AGAIN IN 1910 TO CHARLOTTESVILLE, VIRGINIA AND STUDY DRAWING AT THE UNIVERSITY OF VIRGINIA. IN 1916 ALFRED STIEGLITZ WAS MADE AWARE OF HER ART, IMPRESSED BY HER TALENT HE EXHIBITED SOME OF HER WORK. IN 1918 O'KEEFFE, MOVING BACK TO N.Y. CITY, BECAME A PART OF A GROUP OF PROGRESSIVE ARTISTS AND IN 1924 O'KEEFFE MARRIED ALFRED STIEGLITZ AND WOULD SPEND HER TIME BETWEEN NEW YORK CITY AND THE UPSTATE STIEGLITZ FAMILY HOME AT LAKE GEORGE. IN 1929 HAVING SPENT PART OF A SUMMER IN NEW MEXICO, GEORGIA O'KEEFFE WOULD CONTINUE TO DO SO THROUGH THE YEARS. IN 1949 THREE YEARS AFTER HER HUSBAND DIED SHE MOVED TO NEW MEXICO WHERE SHE CONTINUED TO PRODUCE HER SIMPLE, BOLD, UNMATCHED WORKS OF ART UNTIL HER DEATH.

ROCKWELL KENT

ROCKWELL KENT (1882-1971), ILLUSTRATOR, PAINTER, AUTHOR, ARCHITECT, AND DESIGNER, CAME TO THE ADIRONDACKS IN 1927, PURCHASED 200 ACRES NEAR AUSABLE FORKS AND BUILT A HOUSE, STUDIO AND BARN. HE FOUND TRANQUILITY ON HIS FARM, ASGAARD (ICELANDIC FOR "AN EARTHLY PARADISE") AND DID MANY DRAMATIC ADIRONDACK LANDSCAPE OIL PAINTINGS. DURING HIS EARLY LIFE HE WORKED AS AN ARCHITECTURAL DRAFTSMAN, LOBSTERMAN, AND SHIP'S CARPENTER. HIS POPULAR TRAVEL BOOKS DESCRIBE JOURNEYS TO MAINE, NEWFOUNDLAND, ALASKA, GREENLAND AND TIERRA DEL FUEGO. KENT WAS NOTED FOR HIS DRAMATIC PEN AND INK ILLUSTRATIONS FOR SUCH BOOKS AS "MOBY DICK." ALTHOUGH HE WAS NOT A COMMUNIST, HE WAS AN OUTSPOKEN LEFTIST AND WAS ATTACKED BY SENATOR McCARTHY, WHICH LED KENT TO DONATE MUCH OF HIS ART TO THE SOVIET UNION. IN 1969 A FIRE DESTROYED HIS HOME BUT KENT AND HIS WIFE RESTORED IT. HE IS BURIED ON ASGAARD FARM OVERLOOKING HIS BELOVED WHITEFACE MT. SOME OF HIS BEST ADIRONDACK WORK IS AT THE PLATTSBURGH STATE ART MUSEUM.

THE DRIFTER, BY

ROCKWELL KENT

Seneca Ray
1843 STODDARD 1917

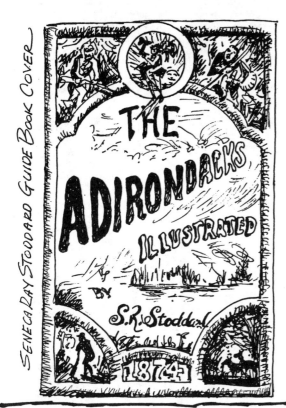

SENECA RAY STODDARD GUIDE BOOK COVER

SENECA RAY STODDARD WAS NOTED FOR HIS SUPERB PHOTOGRAPHY, BEST SELLING GUIDEBOOKS, MAPS, HARD-HITTING EDITORIALS, AND LECTURES ON THE MAGNIFICENT BEAUTY AND RECREATIONAL OPPORTUNITIES OF THE ADIRONDACK MOUNTAINS. HE GREW UP ON A FARM NEAR WILTON AND MOVED TO TROY WHERE HE LEARNED DECORATIVE PAINTING OF RAILWAY CARRIAGES. IN 1864 HE MOVED TO GLEN FALLS, CONTINUED AS A SIGN PAINTER, AND LEARNED PHOTOGRAPHY. HE TRAVELED THROUGHOUT THE ADIRONDACKS PHOTOGRAPHING THE MOUNTAINS, LAKES, HOTELS, GUIDES, LOGGERS, HUNTERS, AND THE TOURISTS. STODDARD PUBLISHED GUIDEBOOKS ILLUSTRATED WITH PHOTOGRAPHS THAT DREW MANY TOURISTS. HE GAVE LECTURES ILLUSTRATED WITH IMAGES, POETRY, FACTS, AND HUMOR. HE DEFENDED THE ADIRONDACKS AGAINST THE LOGGING INDUSTRY AND DEVELOPERS. HIS WORK INFLUENCED THE CREATION OF THE ADIRONDACK PARK AND THE IDEA OF KEEPING IT "FOREVER WILD."

© MARTY PODSKOCH - SAM GLANZMAN 2005

HENRY M. BEACH

LAKE BONAPA
REMSEN N.Y.

1857
LOWVILLE

WE CAUGHT SEVERAL OF
PHOTO BY H.M. BEACH REM

GRANT, N.Y. PO

HENRY M. BEACH (1863-1943) WAS
A PROLIFIC PHOTOGRAPHER WHO FO-
CUSED ON THE WESTERN ADIRONDACKS
DURING THE EARLY 20TH CENTURY.
FROM HIS HOME NEAR LOWVILLE AND
LATER REMSEN, BEACH ROAMED THE
WESTERN ADIRONDACK REGION ON
HORSE, BY TRAIN, AND LATER BY
AUTOMOBILE PHOTOGRAPHING TRAIN
STATIONS, HUNTING AND LUMBER CAMPS, PAPER MILLS, MINES, HOTELS,
LANDSCAPE SCENES, AND SCHOOLS. BEACH ALSO PRODUCED AND
SOLD THOUSANDS OF PHOTO POST CARDS THAT SHOWED THE DECLINE
OF THE HORSE AND BUGGY ERA, AND THE RISE OF THE AUTOMOBILE
THAT BROUGHT A FLOOD OF TOURISTS TO THE ADIRONDACKS.

© 2005 MARTY PODSKOCH - SAM GLANZMAN

1815 MOTHER JOHNSON 1875

DURING THE 1860s AND 1870s, LUCY JOHNSON AND HER HUSBAND PHILANDER RAN THE POPULAR MOTHER JOHNSON'S INN AT RAQUETTE FALLS NORTH OF LONG LAKE. THE JOHNSONS FIRST CAME THERE AND WORKED IN A LUMBER CAMP BUT WHEN IT CLOSED, THEY BECAME INKEEPERS. THEY HELPED TRANSPORT BAGGAGE AROUND THE TWO-MILE CARRY ON THE RAQUETTE RIVER. REV. WILLIAM H.H. "ADIRONDACK" MURRAY VISITED THE INN AND SAID SHE WAS A DELIGHTFUL, GOOD-NATURED PERSON AND A GREAT COOK. "NEVER GO BY WITHOUT TASTING HER PANCAKES." ANOTHER TRAVELER SAID HE ASKED HER. "WHAT KIND OF FISH SHE HAD SERVED HIM?" "WELL", SHE SAID, "THEY DON'T HAVE NAMES AFTER THE 15th OF SEPTEMBER. THEY ARE A GOOD DEAL LIKE TROUT, BUT IT'S AGAINST THE LAW TO CATCH TROUT AFTER THE FIFTEENTH, YOU KNOW."

© MARTY PODSKOCH - SAM GLANZMAN 2005

HENRY VAN HOEVENBERG'S ADIRONDACK LODGE

HENRY VAN HOEVENBERG (1849–1918), A WEALTHY INVENTOR, WOODSMAN, AND HOTEL HOST, BUILT A GIGANTIC HOTEL, A FEW MILES SOUTH OF LAKE PLACID IN 1880. THE ADIRONDACK LODGE WAS AN 85' X 36' THREE-STORY SPRUCE LOG BUILDING WITH A 70' TOWER ON HEART LAKE WHERE HE AND HIS LATE GIRLFRIEND, JOSEPHINE SCOFIELD, HAD PLANNED A HOME. IT WAS THE LARGEST LOG BUILDING IN THE US. GUESTS LOVED MR. VAN FOR HIS STORYTELLING AND GUIDED HIKES OVER 50 MILES OF TRAILS. DURABLE LEATHER PANTS AND JACKETS WERE HENRY'S TRADEMARK ATTIRE. IN 1895 VAN LOST THE LODGE DUE TO LAWSUITS TO HIS PATENTS BUT RETURNED IN 1900 AS MANAGER FOR THE LAKE PLACID CLUB. A HUGE FOREST FIRE IN 1903 FORCED VAN FROM THE LODGE BUT HE RETURNED. A DEVOTED WORKER PERSUADED HIM TO LEAVE. BY NIGHT THEY REACHED INDIAN PASS, AND SADLY HEARD THE THUNDEROUS CRASHING OF HIS BELOVED LODGE.

2007 © MARTY PODSKOCH – SAM GLANZMAN

PROSPECT HOUSE

IN 1881 FREDERIC DURANT, NEPHEW OF THE UNION PACIFIC RAIL-ROAD TYCOON, THOMAS C. DURANT, BUILT THE SIX-STORY PROSPECT HOUSE ON BLUE MOUNTAIN LAKE. IT WAS THE FIRST HOTEL IN THE WORLD TO HAVE ELECTRIC LIGHT IN ALL 300 ROOMS.

PROSPECT HOUSE HAD A STEAM-POWERED HYDRAULIC ELEVATOR, RUNNING WATER, A TWO-STORY OUTHOUSE, BOWLING ALLEYS, BILLIARD ROOMS, GOLF LINKS, LAWN TENNIS, SWIMMING, BOAT RIDES, SHOOTING GALLERY, A RESTAURANT, A LIBRARY, A PHYSICIAN AND PHARMACY, A TELEGRAPH OFFICE, STEAM HEAT, HUNTING AND FISHING, AND A RESIDENT ORCHESTRA.

THE ASTORS, TIFFANYS, VANDERBILTS, MACYS, AND ROOSEVELTS TRAVELED 10 HOURS FROM NYC BY THE NY CENTRAL OR D & H RAILROADS AND THEN ENDURED AN ARDUOUS JOURNEY BY BOAT AND STAGECOACH BEFORE ARRIVING AT THIS PALACE IN THE WILDERNESS. IT WAS CONSIDERED THE MOST FASHIONABLE MOUNTAIN HOTEL IN THE NORTHERN UNITED STATES.

ST. HUBERT'S INN

ST. HUBERT'S INN, A 4-STORY HOTEL BUILT IN 1890 IN KEENE VALLEY, IS THE SOCIAL CENTER OF THE AUSABLE CLUB AND ADIRONDACK MOUNTAIN RESERVE (AMR). ON THIS SITE IN 1876 SMITH BEEDE HAD PURCHASED 600 WILDER — NESS ACRES FOR 2,000 BUSHELS OF WHEAT AND BUILT BEEDE'S HOUSE (A HOTEL). THAT BECAME A TOURIST MECCA. IN 1890 BEEDE AND SON ORLANDO SOLD IT TO AMR, BUT BE- FORE THE DEED WAS TRANSFERRED, THE HOTEL BURNED, AMR ALREADY OWNED A 28,000 -ACRE PRESERVE NEARBY AND UPPER AND LOWER AUSABLE LAKES. THEY BUILT A NEW HO- TEL AND NAMED IT ST. HUBERT'S (C. 657-727), THE PATRON SAINT OF HUNTERS. IN 1978 AMR SOLD ALL THEIR HIGH PEAKS LAND TO THE STATE BUT SAVED 7,000 -ACRES WHERE HUNTING IS PROHIBITED AND HIKING IS OPEN TO THE PUBLIC.

HUBERT, A RECKLESS YOUNG MAN SAW A STAG WITH A CRUCIFIX BETWEEN HIS ANTLERS. HE HEARD A VOICE SCOLDING HIM FOR BEING RUTHLESS AND ASKING FOR COMPASSION. HUBERT GAVE UP HIS LAND AND TITLES, JOINED THE CHURCH AND BECAME AN ARDENT GAME PROTECTOR.

ST. HUBERT, PATRON SAINT OF HUNTING, SHOOTING AND FISHING WAS BORN IN THE MIDDLE OF THE 7th CENTURY A.D.

GLANZMAN

© 2006 - MARTY PODSKOCH - SAM

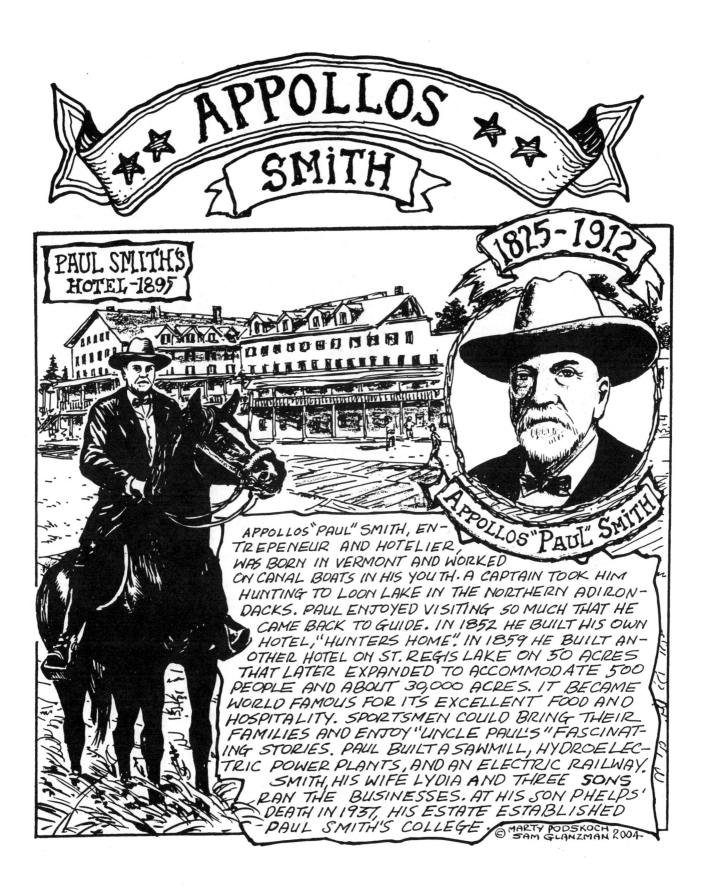

APPOLLOS SMITH

1825–1912

PAUL SMITH'S HOTEL - 1895

APPOLLOS "PAUL" SMITH

APPOLLOS "PAUL" SMITH, ENTREPENEUR AND HOTELIER, WAS BORN IN VERMONT AND WORKED ON CANAL BOATS IN HIS YOUTH. A CAPTAIN TOOK HIM HUNTING TO LOON LAKE IN THE NORTHERN ADIRONDACKS. PAUL ENJOYED VISITING SO MUCH THAT HE CAME BACK TO GUIDE. IN 1852 HE BUILT HIS OWN HOTEL, "HUNTERS HOME". IN 1859 HE BUILT ANOTHER HOTEL ON ST. REGIS LAKE ON 50 ACRES THAT LATER EXPANDED TO ACCOMMODATE 500 PEOPLE AND ABOUT 30,000 ACRES. IT BECAME WORLD FAMOUS FOR ITS EXCELLENT FOOD AND HOSPITALITY. SPORTSMEN COULD BRING THEIR FAMILIES AND ENJOY "UNCLE PAUL'S" FASCINATING STORIES. PAUL BUILT A SAWMILL, HYDROELECTRIC POWER PLANTS, AND AN ELECTRIC RAILWAY. SMITH, HIS WIFE LYDIA AND THREE SONS RAN THE BUSINESSES. AT HIS SON PHELPS' DEATH IN 1937, HIS ESTATE ESTABLISHED PAUL SMITH'S COLLEGE.

© MARTY PODSKOCH
SAM GLANZMAN 2004

LAKE PLACID CLUB

MELVIL DEWEY, FOUNDER OF THE AMERICAN LIBRARY ASSOCIATION AND INVENTOR OF THE DEWEY DECIMAL SYSTEM FOR CLASSIFYING BOOKS, FIRST CAME TO THE ADIRONDACKS IN THE 1890s TO RELIEVE HAY FEVER. HE FOLLOWED PAUL SMITH'S ADVICE AND BEGAN THE LAKE PLACID CLUB ON MIRROR LAKE IN THE VILLAGE OF LAKE PLACID IN 1895. DEWEY ONLY WANTED THE "BEST" PEOPLE AROUND HIM SO HE RESTRICTED ITS MEMBERSHIP. ONLY "PROMINENT CITIZENS" COULD APPLY. THE CLUB GREW TO COVER TWO SQUARE MILES WITH HOTELS, COTTAGES, SCHOOLS, TENNIS COURTS, GOLF COURSES, GARDENS, CONCERT HALLS, STRETCHES OF WILDERNESS, AND ITS OWN FIRE DEPARTMENT. TWENTY-SIX FARMS PROVIDED FRESH FOOD FOR MEMBERS. HIS SON, GODFREY, PROMOTED WINTER SPORTS BY MAKING SKATING RINKS, BRINGING SKI INSTRUCTORS FROM NORWAY, AND BUILDING A SKI JUMP. GODFREY WAS CREDITED WITH BRINGING THE 1932 WINTER OLYMPICS TO LAKE PLACID.

© 2005 MARTY POOSKOCH / SAM GLANZMAN

1851   1931

MELVIL DEWEY

SKI-JORING ON MIRROR LAKE IN FRONT OF THE MAIN CLUB HOUSE

DR. EWARD LIVINGSTON TRUDEAU, M.D.

AFTER CARING FOR HIS BROTHER WHO HAD DIED FROM TUBERCULOSIS, EDWARD LIVINGSTON TRUDEAU ENROLLED IN THE COLLEGE OF PHYSICIANS AND SURGEONS IN NEW YORK AND DEVOTED HIMSELF TO WORKING WITH TB PATIENTS. HE CAME DOWN WITH TB HIMSELF, AND EXPECTING TO DIE, WENT TO HIS FAVORITE RESORT, PAUL SMITH'S HOTEL IN THE NORTHERN ADIRONDACKS, WHERE HE REGAINED HIS HEALTH IN THE MOUNTAIN AIR. IN 1885, TRUDEAU BUILT A "CURE COTTAGE," CALLED "LITTLE RED," NEAR SARANAC. BY 1900 IT WAS A 22-BUILDING COMPLEX WHERE TRUDEAU PRESCRIBED EXERCISE, ISOLATION, REST, GOOD FOOD, AND SLEEPING ON OUTDOOR PORCHES. THE SARANAC LAKE RESORT ACHIEVED GREAT SUCCESS IN HELPING TB PATIENTS.

1848-1915

"LITTLE RED" AT SARANAC LAKE, THE FIRST REST HOME FOR TB PATIENTS IN THE UNITED STATES.

© MARTY PODSKOCH — SAM GLANZMAN — 2005

ROBERT LOUIS STEVENSON, THE SCOTTISH AUTHOR OF TREASURE ISLAND AND THE STRANGE CASE OR DR. JEKYLL AND MR. HYDE, CAME TO THE U.S. IN 1887 TO SEEK TREATMENT FOR HIS PULMONARY ILLNESS. HE WENT TO SARANAC LAKE FOR HELP FROM DR. TRUDEAU'S WORLD FAMOUS ADIRONDACK COTTAGE SANITORIUM. HE AND HIS FAMILY SPENT THE WINTER IN THE BAKER COTTAGE. HIS WIFE, FANNY, WROTE, "(ROBERT) IS NOW MORE LIKE A HARDY MOUNTAINEER, TAKING LONG WALKS ON HILL TOPS IN ALL SEASONS AND WEATHER."

ROBERT STEVENSON ALSO WROTE ESSAYS AND BEGAN WRITING "THE MASTER OF BALLANTRAE." THE OUTDOOR EXERCISE, NOURSHING FOOD AND ADIRONDACK AIR IMPROVED HIS HEALTH. AFTER SIX MONTHS HE WENT TO THE SAMOAN ISLANDS WHERE HE DIED.

© 2004 MARTY PODSKOCH - SAM GLANZMAN

TODAY, THE LARGEST COLLECTION OF STEVENSON'S MEMORABILIA IS ON DISPLAY AT STEVENSON'S COTTAGE AND MUSEUM IN SARANAC LAKE.

THEODORE ROOSEVELT

"COMPLICATED, COMPLICATED, BUT I DON'T WANT TO BECOME PRESIDENT THROUGH A GRAVE YARD. I WOULD RATHER WORK FOR IT."

ON FRIDAY THE 13TH OF SEPTEMBER 1901, VICE PRESIDENT "TEDDY" ROOSEVELT WHILE VACATIONING AT THE TAHAWUS CLUB NEAR NEWCOMB CLIMBED MT. MARCY. A GUIDE BROUGHT A MESSAGE THAT PRESIDENT MCKINLEY WAS DYING FROM AN ASSASSIN'S BULLET IN BUFFALO. THAT NIGHT TEDDY WAS DRIVEN 35 MILES IN A HORSE DRAWN WAGON OVER TORTUOUS, MUDDY, WASHED OUT ROADS. MIKE CRONIN DROVE THE LAST 16 MILES IN ONE HOUR AND 41 MINUTES WITH TEDDY HOLDING A LANTERN TO GUIDE MIKE. AT DAWN THEY ARRIVED AT THE NORTH CREEK RAILROAD WHERE TEDDY LEARNED THAT MCKINLEY HAD DIED AT 2:15 AM. TEDDY BECAME PRESIDENT OF THE UNITED STATES AT THE AGE OF FORTY-TWO. A WAITING TRAIN TOOK TEDDY TO BUFFALO WHERE HE WAS SWORN IN THAT EVENING.

BENJAMIN — HARRISON'S SUMMER HOME

BENJAMIN HARRISON (1833-1901), GRANDSON OF US PRES. WILLIAM HARRISON AND 23ᴰ U.S. PRES. (1889-1893), BUILT A SUMMER RETREAT, "BERKELEY LODGE," IN 1896 ON 37 ACRES BETWEEN FIRST AND SECOND LAKES ON THE FULTON CHAIN. HERE HE ES-CAPED NEWSPAPER REPORTERS TO WRITE, HUNT, FISH, AND RELAX WITH HIS FRIENDS AND FAMILY. HE SAID "OLD FORGE, NY IS A BEAUTIFUL AND DELIGHTFUL REGION." THE LODGE HAD A LIVING ROOM FLANKED BY TWIN OCTAGONAL TOWERS. A COTTAGE WITH A KITCHEN, DINING ROOM, AND OFFICE WAS AT-TACHED. THERE WAS ALSO A BOATHOUSE AND A HOUSE FOR GUIDES. IN 1896 HARRISON (62), A WIDOWER MARRIED HIS WIFE'S SISTER'S DAUGH-TER, MARY DIMMICK (38) AND THEY HAD A DAUGH-TER, ELIZABETH. HE MINGLED WITH THE LOCAL RESIDENTS, ATTENDED THE PRESBYTERIAN CHURCH, AND ENJOYED CHICKEN AND BISCUITS AT THE BALD MOUNTAIN HOUSE ON THIRD LAKE. THE FIRST MAIL BOAT SERVICE IN THE U.S. WAS BEGUN TO BRING HIS MAIL.

HARRISON SPENT SEVEN SUMMERS AT BERKELEY LODGE, BEFORE HIS DEATH IN 1901.

© 2006 - MARTY PODSKOCH - SAM GLANZMAN

A DAY'S BAG OF DUCKHUNTING

MOSES COHEN
OLD FORGE HARDWARE

MOSES COHEN (1870-1961), THE FOUNDER OF THE OLD FORGE HARDWARE (AKA "THE MILLION ITEM STORE"), CAME FROM LITHUANIA (1886) TO LIVE WITH HIS BROTHER, DAVID, IN DANNEMORA. THEY OPENED A HARDWARE STORE IN BLOOMINGDALE AND LATER IN SARANAC LAKE. THE BUSSINESS COULDN'T SUPPORT TWO STORES, SO, MOSES BECAME A PEDDLER WALKING FROM FARMS AND VILLAGES WITH TWO PACKS WEIGHING ABOUT 100 LBS: A BACK PACK THAT WENT DOWN TO HIS CALVES CONTAINED CLOTHING, TABLECLOTHS, COOKWARE AND OTHER HOUSEHOLD ITEMS, AND A VALISE CONTAINED STOCKINGS AND SEWING ITEMS. HE BOUGHT A HORSE AND WAGON BUT WHEN THE HORSE DIED HE WENT BACK TO WALKING. AFTER PEDDLING FOR A FEW YEARS, MOSES HEARD THAT OLD FORGE NEEDED A HARDWARE STORE AND IN 1888 HE OPENED ONE IN THE BASEMENT OF THE FORGE HOUSE. HE LATER BUILT A 3-STORY BUILDING THAT BURNED IN 1920 AND WAS REBUILT IN 1922.

© 2006 MARTY PODSKOCH — SAM GLANZMAN

BETH JOSEPH SYNAGOGUE

BETH JOSEPH SYNAGOGUE IN TUPPER LAKE, THE OLDEST SYNA-
GOGUE IN THE ADIRONDACKS, COMPLETED IN 1905, WAS BUILT BY JEWISH
IMMIGRANTS FROM RUSSIA AND EASTERN EUROPE. THEY WERE ITINERANT
PEDDLERS (HENCE IT'S POPULAR NAME: THE "PEDDLERS SYNAGOGUE")
CARRYING 60-POUND PACKS OF CLOTH, NEEDLES AND HOUSEHOLD
GOODS. THE CONGREGATION HELD SERVICES IN THEIR HOMES. THEY PLAN-
NED A $3,500 MODEST WOOD FRAME BUILDING WITH PEWS AND WOOD
STOVE FUNDED BY YEAR-ROUND AND SUMMER JEWISH RESIDENTS AND
SOME NON-JEWISH BUSINESSMEN. THE SYNAGOGUE HAD BEAUTI-
FUL WAINSCOT CEILING AND WALLS AND TWO ROUND ROSE STAINED-
GLASS WINDOWS. THERE WAS A RABBI TO TEACH THE CHILDREN AND
ALSO A KOSHER BUTCHER. THE SYNAGOGUE WAS CLOSED ABOUT
1960 BUT IN 1987 LOCAL RESIDENTS BEGAN RAISING MONEY TO
RESTORE THE TEMPLE. IT REOPENED IN 1990 AND TODAY IS OPEN
TO THE PUBLIC DURING THE SUMMER MONTHS.

Beth Joseph Synagogue
Early 1900's

© 2006 MARTY PODSKOCH — SAM GLADZMAN

FRED E. VAILLANCOURT

FRED E. VAILLANCOURT WAS A WELL-KNOWN ADIRONDACK ITINERANT PEDDLER IN THE EARLY 20TH C. HE HAD BEEN A BRAKEMAN ON THE GRAND TRUNK RAILROAD IN 1907 IN MAINE WHEN HE LOST HIS LEFT LEG AND MOST OF HIS RIGHT. UNDAUNTED, FRED USED SHORTENED CRUTCHES AND THE STUMP OF HIS RIGHT LEG TO GET AROUND. HE WAS A FAMILY MAN SO HE BECAME A PEDDLER OF NOVELTIES AND POST-CARDS MANY OF WHICH WERE OF HIM. HE WOULD TRAVEL DOOR TO DOOR IN TOWNS, FARMS AND LOGGING CAMPS. HIS ROUTE BEGAN IN WAR-RENSBURG AND EXTENDED ABOUT 40 MILES TO INDIAN LAKE. DURING THE WINTER FRED RODE IN A SPECIALLY FITTED SLEIGH PULLED BY TWO LARGE DOGS. DURING THE REST OF THE YEAR HE RODE IN A WAGON. EVERYONE IN THE TOWNS AND LUMBER CAMPS KNEW FRED AS A FRIENDLY CHEERFUL PERSON. FRED SAID THAT ADIRONDACK PEOPLE ALWAYS TREATED HIM WITH KINDNESS. ONE DAY, HOW-EVER, ONE OF FRED'S DOGS ATTACKED HIM. FORTUNATELY FRED'S OTHER DOG THREW HIM-SELF INTO THE FRAY KILLING HIS MATE AND RESCUING HIS CRIPPLED MASTER.

©2006 MARTY PODSKOCH ~SAM GLAZZMAN

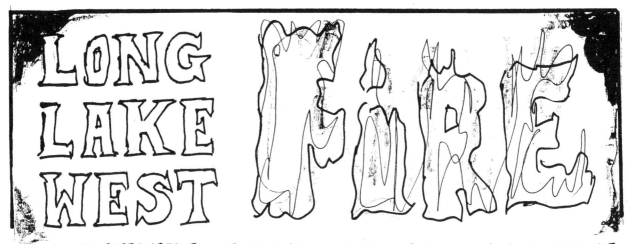

LONG LAKE WEST FIRE

ON SEPTEMBER 9, 1908 A MOHAWK AND MALONE LOCOMOTIVE IGNITED THE DRY KINDLING ALONG THE TRACKS NEAR LONG LAKE WEST, NOW SABATTIS. ABOUT 150 MEN DUG MILES OF TRENCHES AND FINALLY CONTAINED THE FIRE BUT ON SEPTEMBER 26, STRONG WINDS FANNED THE FIRE AROUND THE FIRE-BREAK AND ROARED TOWARDS LONG LAKE WEST. THERE THE RAILROAD AGENT TELEGRAPHED TUPPER LAKE (19 MILES NORTH) AND A RELIEF TRAIN CAME. SURVIVOR ART JENNINGS SAID, "THERE WERE ABOUT 100 PEOPLE IN THE TOWN AND MOST WERE LUMBERJACKS. ALL THE FEMALES GOT ON FIRST. MY MOTHER, MARGARET CARRIED ME ON. THERE WAS ONE GUY WHO CRAWLED INTO A BOXCAR. THERE WAS A KEG IN THE CAR AND HE TAPPED IT, MAYBE THAT SAVED HIS LIFE." THE RESCUE TRAIN PLOWED THROUGH SMOKE AND FLAMES THAT SCORCHED AND BLISTERED THE CARS. PEOPLE IN TUPPER LAKE HEARD A TREMENDOUS BOOM WHEN A BUILDING CONTAINING 1,300 LBS. OF DYNAMITE EXPLODED.

©2006 MARTY PODSKOCH
SAM GLANZMAN

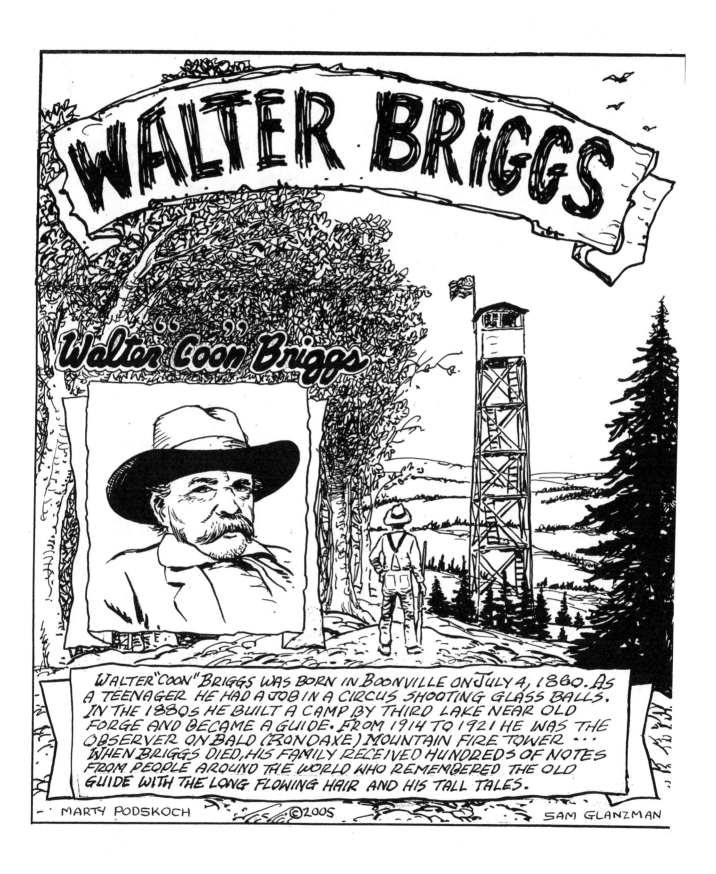

WALTER "COON" BRIGGS WAS BORN IN BOONVILLE ON JULY 4, 1860. AS A TEENAGER HE HAD A JOB IN A CIRCUS SHOOTING GLASS BALLS. IN THE 1880s HE BUILT A CAMP BY THIRD LAKE NEAR OLD FORGE AND BECAME A GUIDE. FROM 1914 TO 1921 HE WAS THE OBSERVER ON BALD (RONDAXE) MOUNTAIN FIRE TOWER ··· WHEN BRIGGS DIED, HIS FAMILY RECEIVED HUNDREDS OF NOTES FROM PEOPLE AROUND THE WORLD WHO REMEMBERED THE OLD GUIDE WITH THE LONG FLOWING HAIR AND HIS TALL TALES.

MARTY PODSKOCH ©2005 SAM GLANZMAN

SAM CHEETHAM

1886
1953

SAM CHEETHAM OVER-
CAME TUBERCULOSIS AND
BECAME A FIRE OBSERVER
ON WHITEFACE MOUNTAIN.
   AFTER HE CONTRACTED
TB IN HARTFORD, SAM CAME
TO SARANAC LAKE TO BE
CURED. AT THE TIME HE
COULD ONLY CLIMB STAIRS
ON HIS HANDS AND KNEES
BUT WAS SO FASCINATED WITH
WHITEFACE MOUNTAIN, WHICH
HE COULD SEE FROM HIS
ROOM, HE VOWED TO CLIMB
ITS PEAK. A VIGOROUS
LIFE OF WALKING AND
WORKING OUTSIDE HEALED
HIM AND HE BECAME THE
WHITEFACE OBSERVER
(1915-19, AND 1934-42).
   HE CLIMBED THE 6½
MILE TRAIL TO THE SUM-
MIT WITH A HEAVY PACK.
AT FIRST, SINCE THERE
WAS NO TOWER, SAM HAD
JUST A TENT WITH A WOOD
STOVE ON THE SUMMIT. IN
1919 SAM GOT A 22 FT.
STEEL TOWER, WITH A CAB,
WHICH PROTECTED HIM.
WHEN THE WEATHER STA-
TION WAS BUILT IN 1937,
SAM BECAME THE WINTER
OBSERVER AND RADIO OP-
ERATOR AND LIVED ON THE
MOUNTAIN THAT HE LOVED
YEAR-ROUND.

© 2005 MARTY PODSKOCH - SAM GLANZMAN

THE AMPERSAND HERMIT

WALTER CHANNING RICE (1851-1924)

WALTER CHANNING RICE, "THE AMPERSAND HERMIT," BEGAN WORKING AT PAUL SMITH'S HOTEL IN 1867 AS A HANDYMAN AND GUIDE. IN 1887 HE BUILT AND RAN A BOARDING HOUSE, THE VILLA DORSEY, NEAR SARANAC LAKE. HE WAS THE FIRE OBSERVER ON AMPERSAND MOUNTAIN FROM 1915 TO 1923 AND BUILT A STONE HUT ON THE SUMMIT AND READ THE CLASSICS. HIKERS GOT A GREAT VIEW, GOOD STORIES, AND WORDS OF WISDOM. "I NEVER FOUND IT LONESOME ON AMPERSAND FOR I HAVE FRIENDS UP THERE. I HAVE A FEATHERED ORCHESTRA TO WAKEN ME IN THE MORNING AND HEDGEHOGS WHO COME MOST INFORMALLY TO VISIT ME AT NIGHT... THE SQUIRRELS CHATTERS NONSENSE AT ME AND OCCASIONALLY A DEER LOOKS AT ME IN AMAZEMENT."

ON AMPERSAND MOUNTAIN, THERE IS A PLAQUE ON THE SUMMIT THAT STATES, "IN LOVING MEMORY OF WALTER CHANNING RICE, "HERMIT OF AMPERSAND," WHO KEPT VIGIL FROM THIS PEAK, 1915-1923." ©2004 MARTY PODSKOCH SAM GLANZMAN

FRANCES BOONE SEAMAN

IN 1942, AT THE AGE OF 23, FRANCES BECAME THE FIRE TOWER OBSERVER ON ROCK MOUNTAIN (LATER CALLED MOUNT ELECTRA) IN "NEHASANE PARK," THE 40,000-ACRE ESTATE OF DR. W. SEWARD WEBB. THE 70' TOWER WAS A DAUNTING CLIMB AND TOOK SOME GETTING USED TO, BUT FRANCES BICYCLED 3/4 OF A MILE FROM HER CABIN IN GREEN VALLEY, HIKED ANOTHER MILE EVERY DAY TO THE TOWER, AND CLIMBED ALOFT TO SCAN FOR SMOKE. IN HER FREE TIME SHE WROTE, DREW, READ, AND PRACTICED HER SKILL WITH BOW AN ARROW. SHE ONCE MET A BEAR AND HER CUB ON THE WAY TO THE PRIVY, AND WAS STARTLED BY THE SCREAMS OF A PANTHER. SHE WORKED ALONE AND LONGED FOR HER BOYFRIEND, HOWARD, WHO WAS IN SERVICE. WHEN HE RETURNED, THEY GOT MARRIED AND LIVED IN LONG LAKE.

©2004
MARTY PODSKOCH
SAM GLANZMAN

ADIRONDACK LEAGUE CLUB

"MOUNTAIN LODGE" CLUB HOUSE ON MOOSE LAKE

IN 1890 THE ADIRONDACK LEAGUE CLUB, A PRIVATE LANDOWNERS' ORGANIZATION WAS FOUNDED TO CREATE A HUNTING, FISHING AND RECREATION PRESERVE FOR ITS MEMBERS EAST OF OLD FORGE IN HAMILTON COUNTY. BY 1893 THE ALC OWNED OR HELD HUNTING RIGHTS TO ABOUT 200,000 ACRES OF FOREST AND LAKES, NEARLY 40 MILES WIDE AND 25 MILES LONG. THERE WERE THREE LAKE COMMUNITIES WHERE CLUB MEMBERS OWNED THEIR LOTS AND CAMPS. THE LAKES STILL HAVE LODGES FOR ENTERTAINING, INDOOR ACTIVITIES, AND ROOM AND BOARD. ARCHITECT AUGUSTUS D. SHEPARD DESIGNED MANY OF THE CAMP DWELLINGS. THE LARGEST AND GRANDEST, MOUNTAIN LODGE, HAS MASSIVE LOG BEAMS AND A STONE FIREPLACE. SHEPARD'S RUSTIC BUILDINGS INFLUENCED THE DESIGN OF NATIONAL PARK SERVICE STRUCTURES. TODAY THE CLUB ENCOURAGES GOOD STEWARDSHIP BY PRACTICING WILDLIFE AND RESOURCE MANAGEMENT ON ITS 50,000 ARCES.

© 2005 MARTY PODSKOCH — SAM GLANZMAN

THE ASSOCIATION FOR THE PROTECTION OF THE ADIRONDACKS

THE ASSOCIATION FOR THE PROTECTION OF THE ADIRONDACKS WAS THE FIRST ORGANIZED ADVOCATE FOR THE ADIRONDACKS, CREATED IN 1901 BY ADIRONDACK LANDOWNERS IN NYC WHO WERE WORRIED THAT THE STATE WOULD ALLOW BUSINESS TO DESTROY FOREST PRESERVE LAND. GIFFORD PINCHOT, A PROMINENT U.S. FORESTER, HAD URGED THE STATE TO REPEAL ARTICLE 14, THE "FOREVER WILD CLAUSE" OF THE NYS CONSTITUTION THAT PRESERVED WILDERNESS ON STATE LAND. HE DREW UP A COLORED MAP OF 100,000 ACRES OF VIRGIN FOREST AROUND RAQUETTE LAKE TO BE 'SCIENTIFICALLY' LOGGED WITH SIGNIFICANT DEVELOPMENT OF ROADS AND BUILDINGS. THE ASSOCIATION PERSUADED THE LEGISLATURE TO REJECT THE PLAN AND KEEP ARTICLE 14, THEIR FIRST VICTORY. BETWEEN 1906 AND 1955 THEY SUCCESSFULLY FOUGHT PROPOSALS TO DAM ADIRONDACK RIVERS. TODAY, THE ASSOCIATION HAS ITS OFFICE AND PUBLIC ACCESSIBLE RESEARCH LIBRARY IN NISKAYUNA, WHERE IT CONTINUES TO MONITOR ILLEGAL CUTTING OF TREES BY STATE DEPARTMENTS, TO OPPOSE MEGA-RESORT DEVELOPMENT AND TO PROVIDE ALTERNATIVES THAT AID THE ENVIRONMENT AND LOCAL COMMUNITIES.

© 2007 MARTY PODSKOCH — SAM GLANZMAN

THE CIVILIAN CONSERVATION CORPS (CCC) BEGAN ON MARCH 31, 1933 UNDER PRESIDENT ROOSEVELT'S "NEW DEAL" TO RELIEVE THE POVERTY AND UNEMPLOYMENT OF THE DEPRESSION. THE US ARMY SUPERVISED THE CAMPS WITH 200 MEN EACH. THE FIRST CAMPS WERE SET UP IN THESE ADIRONDACK TOWNS AND COUNTIES: ARIETTA AND SPECULATOR (HAMILTON); BOLTON LANDING (WARREN) TAHAWUS, NEWCOMB, SCHROON RIVER, AND PORT HENRY (ESSEX); WANAKENA AND BENSON MINES (ST. LAWRENCE); PAUL SMITH'S GOLDSMITH'S TUPPER LAKE, LAKE PLACID, AND FISH CREEK POND (FRANKLIN). MEN 18-25 (WITH FATHERS ON RELIEF) ENROLLED FOR 6 MONTHS, WORKED A 40-HOUR WEEK FOR $30/MO. THEY HAD TO SEND $25 A MONTH HOME. THEY GOT GOOD FOOD, UNIFORMS, AND MEDICAL CARE. AT FIRST THEY LIVED IN TENTS; LATER THEY BUILT WOODEN BUILDINGS. WORKERS BUILT TRAILS, ROADS, CAMPSITES, AND DAMS, STOCKED FISH, BUILT AND MAINTAINED FIRE TOWER OBSERVER'S CABINS AND TELEPHONE LINES, FOUGHT FIRES, AND PLANTED MILLIONS OF TREES. THE CCC DISBANDED IN 1942 DUE TO THE NEED FOR MEN IN WWII.

© 2008 MARTY PODSKOCH - SAM GLANZMAN

CLARENCE PETTY

1905

CLARENCE PETTY, ENVIRONMENTALIST AVIATOR AND FLIGHT IN-
STRUCTOR (TILL AGE 94), AND WILDERNESS ADVOCATE FOR THE ADI-
RONDACK PARK, GREW UP WITH TWO BROTHERS, BILL AND ARCHIBALD,
IN THE WILDERNESS NEAR UPPER SARANAC LAKE. HIS FATHER WAS A
GUIDE AND LATER A CARETAKER ON DEER ISLAND. ON SUNDAY AFTERNOONS,
STARTING WHEN CLARENCE WAS 11, HE AND BILL WALKED OR SNOWSHOED 16
MILES TO SARANAC LAKE VILLAGE ON SUNDAYS, WHERE THEY ATTENDED
SCHOOL UNTIL FRIDAY. IN 1930 CLARENCE GRADUATED FROM THE STATE
COLLEGE OF FORESTRY, SYRACUSE. DURING HIS CAREER, CLARENCE SU-
PERVISED A CIVILIAN CONSERVATION CORPS (CCC) CAMP, WAS A WWII PI-
LOT, AND A DISTRICT FOREST RANGER IN ST. LAWRENCE CO. CLARENCE
HIKED, CANOED, AND MAPPED 1,3000 MILES OF ADIRONDACK RIVERS
AND STREAMS. HE HELPED SET UP THE NYS ADIRONDACK PARK AGEN-
CY AND SERVED ON THE BOARD OF THE ADIRONDACK COUNCIL. PETTY SAID,
"IF THINGS GO BAD THE BEST PLACE TO GO IS INTO THE REMOTE WILDER-
NESS. EVERYTHING'S IN BALANCE THERE."

© 2006 MARTY PODSKOCH — SAM GLANZMAN

ESTHER COMBS

ESTHER MOUNTAIN

ESTHER MOUNTAIN (4,270'), THREE MILES NORTH OF WHITEFACE MOUNTAIN, IS THE ONLY HIGH PEAK THAT IS NAMED FOR A WOMAN. IT GOT IT'S NAME FROM A 15-YEAR-OLD FARM GIRL, ESTHER COMBS, WHO LIVED AT THE FOOT OF WHITEFACE MT. SHE ALWAYS DREAMED OF CLIMBING IT FOR ITS GRAND VIEW. HER PARENTS DISCOURAGED HER SAYING, "THE WOODS ARE FULL OF DANGER AND GIRLS SHOULD BE SPINNING AND BAKING." IN 1839 ESTHER SET OUT TO CLIMB WHITEFACE MT. ALONE. SHE PUSHED THROUGH THICK BRUSH AND CLIMBED MANY LEDGES, FINALLY REACHING THE SUMMIT. BUT SHE SOON REALIZED THAT SHE WASN'T ON WHITEFACE BUT RATHER ON AN UNNAMED MOUNTAIN. ESTHER TRIED TO RETURN BUT BECAME LOST AND SPENT THE NIGHT IN THE WOODS. A SEARCH PARTY FOUND HER IN THE MORNING. A PLAQUE ON THE SUMMIT OF ESTHER MOUNTAIN COMMEMORATES HER ASCENT FOR HER "SHEER JOY OF CLIMBING."

© MARTY PODSKOCH – SAM GLANZMAN 2005

ORSON "OLD MOUNTAIN" PHELPS

1817-1905

MT. MARCY

ORSON "OLD MOUNTAIN" PHELPS WAS A NOTED GUIDE, TRAPPER, HUNTER, AND FISHERMAN FROM THE KEENE VALLEY. HE ENJOYED CLIMBING MOUNTAINS, ESPECIALLY "OLD MERCY" (MOUNT MARCY), WHICH HE CLAIMED TO HAVE CLIMBED A HUNDRED TIMES. WHEN CHARLES DUDLEY WARNER, A NOTED WRITER, WROTE ABOUT HIS EXPLOITS AND COLORFUL CHARACTER IN THE "ATLANTIC," PEOPLE FLOCKED TO HIS DOOR. THEY FOUND A MAN WITH SHORT, BOWED LEGS, LONG MATTED HAIR, A HIGH-PITCHED VOICE, AND A FAN-LIKE BEARD, WHO RARELY BATHED. ORSON HAD A PASSIONATE LOVE OF SUNSETS, FORESTS AND THE CHANGING SEASONS AND ENJOYED SHARING NATURE WITH HIS CLIENTS. HE'D SIT ON A LOG, SMOKE HIS PIPE, AND TELL STORIES OF LIFE. PHELPS ALSO WROTE BEAUTIFUL PROSE AND POETRY EXTOLLING THE WONDERS OF NATURE. . . .

© MARTY PODSKOCH – SAM GLANZMAN 2004

ADIRONDACK
MOUNTAIN CLUB

THE ADIRONDACK MOUNTAIN CLUB (ADK) IS AN OUTDOOR CLUB THAT DEVELOPES AND MAINTAINS HIKING TRAILS AND CAMPSITES, PUBLISHES GUIDEBOOKS AND MAPS, AND FOSTERS CONSERVATION EDUCATION. ADK BEGAN AFTER MEADE DOBSON, SECRETARY OF THE NY-NJ TRAIL CONFERENCE, ILLEGALLY CAUGHT A TROUT IN UTICA IN JANUARY 1921 AND BRAGGED TO HIS FRIEND, THE CHIEF GAME PROTECTOR FOR THE CONSERVATION COMMISSION. HE SENT MEADE TO COMMISSIONER GEORGE PRATT WHO LEVIED A MODEST FINE. MEADE THEN TALKED TO THE COMMISSIONER ABOUT THE POOR HIKING SYSTEM IN THE ADIRONDACKS AND SUGGESTED FORMING A CLUB TO CREATE A TRAIL SYSTEM THAT USED OLD LOGGING ROADS. THE PLAN WAS DISCUSSED IN DEC. 1921 IN THE LOG CABIN LUNCHROOM ATOP THE ABERCROMBIE AND FITCH SPORTING GOODS STORE IN NYC. ADK WAS CREATED THE NEXT YEAR. THERE ARE NOW OVER 30,000 MEMBERS IN 27 LOCAL CHAPTERS IN NY, NJ AND MA WORKING TO PROTECT NEW YORK'S FOREST PRESERVE, PARKLANDS AND WATERWAYS.

© 2006 - MARTY PODSKOCH - SAM GLANZMAN

NORTHVILLE PLACID TRAIL

THE NORTHVILLE-PLACID TRAIL (NPT) WAS ONE OF THE FIRST PROJECTS OF THE ADIRONDACK MOUNTAIN CLUB (ADK) IN 1922. IT BEGINS ON THE NORTHERN SHORE OF THE GREAT SACANDAGA LAKE AND THEN IT TRAVELS OVER 130-MILES THROUGH THE WILDERNESS TO LAKE PLACID. ADK LAID OUT THE TRAIL ALONG DIRT ROADS AND LOGGING TRAILS. EARLY HIKERS CAME BY RAILROAD TO NORTHVILLE AND HIKED TO LAKE PLACID WHERE THEY COULD CATCH A TRAIN RIDE HOME. TODAY, THE TRAIL CROSSES A FEW HIGHWAYS WHERE HIKERS CAN REPLENISH THEIR SUPPLIES IN NEARBY VILLAGES. SOME FOLKS SHIP PACKAGES TO POST OFFICES IN PISECO, BLUE MOUNTAIN LAKE, OR LONG LAKE. ONE GALWAY BOY SCOUT RAN THE 133-MILE TRAIL IN 1973 AND A VERMONTER RAN IT IN 37 HOURS AND 31 MINUTES IN 2005. THE AVERAGE HIKER SPENDS 10 DAYS ON THE TRAIL, BUT ONE WHO TAKES 2 WEEKS CAN EXPLORE AND SAVOR THE BEAUTIFUL, TRANQUIL WILD FOREST AND LAKES OF THE ADIRONDACKS.

©2006 MARTY PODSKOCH ~ SAM GLANZMAN

BOB MARSHALL

BOB MARSHALL, FORESTER, AUTHOR, EXPLORER, CONSERVATIONIST, AND CO-FOUNDER OF THE WILDERNESS SOCIETY, WAS ONE OF THE FIRST TO CLIMB THE 46 HIGH PEAKS IN THE ADIRONDACKS. BORN IN NYC WHERE HIS FATHER WAS AN INFLUENTIAL LAWYER AND CONSERVATIONIST, BOB SPENT HIS SUMMERS AT THE FAMILY CAMP, KNOLLWOOD, ON LOWER SARANAC LAKE. IN 1916 BOB (16) AND HIS BROTHER GEORGE (13) SET OUT TO CLIMB THE ADIRONDACK MOUNTAINS OVER 4,000 FEET, MANY WITHOUT TRAILS. HERBERT CLARK GUIDED THEM. IN 1925 THEY CLIMBED THE LAST FOUR. BOB WAS A DIVISION DIRECTOR IN THE U.S. FOREST SERVICE AND MADE FREQUENT 30-40 MILE DAY HIKES. BOB MARSHALL WILDERNESS AREA (MONTANA) AND MOUNT MARSHALL (4,360 FEET) IN THE ADIRONDACKS BEAR HIS NAME. BOB STATED, "TO US THE ENJOYMENT OF SOLITUDE, COMPLETE INDEPENDENCE, AND THE BEAUTY OF UNDEFILED PANORAMAS IS ABSOLUTELY ESSENTIAL TO HAPPINESS.

© 2005 MARTY POOSKOCH SAM GLANZMAN

ADIRONDACK LEAN-TO

THE ADIRONDACK LEAN-TO, A THREE-SIDED ROOFED STRUCTURE, HAS GIVEN HUNTERS, FISHERMEN, TRAPPERS, AND HIKERS PROTECTION FROM THE ELEMENTS FOR NEARLY A HUNDRED YEARS. IT WAS AN IMPROVEMENT OVER THE 'SHANTY,' WHICH EARLY GUIDES MADE OF BARK, SAPLINGS, BOUGHS, AND BRUSH. WHEN GUIDES NEEDED SHELTER, THEY STRIPPED BARK FROM TRESS CAUSING THEM TO DIE. DURING THE LATE 1800s RESORTS SUCH AS VAN HOVENBERGH'S ADIRONDACK LODGE, THE AUSABLE CLUB AND THE LAKE PLACID CLUB BUILT MORE PERMANENT STRUCTURES WITH SPRUCE LOG SIDES, PLANK FLOORS, A SLOPED ROOF EXTENDING OVER THE OPENING, AND BALSAM BOUGHS BEDDING. THE TREES DESTROYED IN MAKING SHANTIES WERE NOW PROTECTED SO THE CONSERVATION DEPT. BUILT THE FIRST ADIRONDACK LEAN-TO IN 1919 WITH STANDARDIZED DIMENSIONS INCLUDING A FIREPLACE IN THE FRONT, A GARBAGE PIT, AND AN OUTHOUSE, 20 MORE WERE ADDED IN 1920. TODAY, THERE ARE ABOUT 235 SUCH LEAN-TOS IN THE ADIRONDACKS.

© 2006 - MARTY PODSKOCK - SAM GLANZMAN

ORRA PHELPS

ORRA "DOC" PHELPS

ADIRONDACK NATURALIST, BOTANIST, PHYSICAN, MOUNTAINEER, TEACHER, AND MENTOR, DEVELOPED A LOVE OF NATURE AS A CHILD EXPLORING THE ADIRONDACKS WITH HER MOTHER. AFTER CLIMBING MOUNT MARCY IN 1924, SHE THEN CLIMBED ALL 46 PEAKS TWICE. CAMPING TO ORRA WAS "A BLANKET ROLL HUNG FROM ONE SHOULDER AND TIED AT THE HIP. INSIDE THE BED ROLL THERE MIGHT BE A CAN OF SOUP, HALF A DOZEN POTATOES, AND A FEW CARROTS." IN 1934, SHE WROTE THE ADIRONDACK MOUNTAIN CLUB'S (ADK) FIRST COMPREHENSIVE TRAIL GUIDE TO THE HIGH PEAKS REGION. ONE NIGHT SHE TRAVELED TO LAKE COLDEN TO TREAT A CAMPER WITH A BADLY SLASHED LEG, PROBABLY THE ONLY DOCTOR TO MAKE A HOUSE CALL AT A LEAN-TO.

ADK 46-R

1895-1986

© MARTY PODSKOCH - SAM GLANZMAN 2005

GRACE LEACH HUDOWALSKI (NO 9)

ADK 46-R

1906
2004

"MOUNTAINS CAN GIVE YOU A LOT IF YOU CAN TAKE THEM"

GRACE HUDOWALSKI, THE FIRST WOMAN TO CLIMB ALL 46 ADIRONDACK HIGH PEAKS, GREW UP IN MINERVA. SHE DISCOVERED THE ADIRONDACK MOUNTAINS WHEN SHE CLIMBED MOUNT MARCY WITH COLLEGE STUDENTS IN 1922. SHE MOVED TO TROY AND MARRIED ED HUDOWALSKI. GRACE GOT HIM INTERESTED IN HIKING THE HIGH PEAKS. ED HELPED START A CHURCH HIKING GROUP THAT BE-CAME THE ADIRONDACK FORTY-SIXERS. GRACE BECAME ITS FIRST PRESIDENT (1940-1942) AND LATER HISTORIAN. SHE CORRESPONDED WITH HIKERS ASPIRING TO CLIMB THE 46 PEAKS OVER 4,000', SOMETIMES WRITING UPWARDS OF 2,000 LETTERS IN ONE YEAR.

FRIENDS CALLED HER "AMAZING GRACE" BECAUSE OF HER ENTHUSIASM AND LOVE FOR CLIMBING. TODAY, ADIRONDACK 46ERS ARE SEEKING TO RENAME EAST DIX, ONE OF THE HIGH PEAKS, "GRACE PEAK" IN HER HONOR.

© MARTY PODSKOCH – SAM GLANZMAN 2005

Noah John Rondeau
1883 – 1967

IN 1929 WHEN HE WAS 46, NOAH JOHN RONDEAU, "NOT WELL SATISFIED WITH THE WORLD AND IT'S TRENDS" BEGAN TO LIVE YEAR-ROUND AT COLD RIVER ALONE AS A HERMIT. OCCASIONALLY HE CAME OUT OF THE WOODS FOR A HOLIDAY OR SUPPLIES. HE BUILT TWO CABINS COVERED WITH TAR PAPER AND CANVAS. ABOUT THE CABINS WERE SIX OR SEVEN WIGWAMS USED FOR SUMMER LIVING AND FIREWOOD. HE HUNTED FISHED, TRAPPED, LOVED TO READ, PLAYED THE VIOLIN AND INSPITE OF LITTLE FORMAL SCHOOLING HIS CAMP HAD OVER SIXTY BOOKS.

MARTY PODSKOCH
SAM GLANZMAN
© 2004

INEZ MILHOLLAND BOISSEVAIN

INEZ MILHOLLAND BOISSEVAIN, A SOCIAL ACTIVIST AND A TOWERING FIGURE IN THE CRUSADE FOR WOMEN'S RIGHTS, SPENT MUCH OF HER EARLY LIFE AT MEADOWMOUNT, THE ANCESTRAL HOME, IN LEWIS IN ESSEX COUNTY. INEZ WAS A MODEL OF THE 'NEW WOMEN' WITH HER DYNAMIC PERSONALITY AND BROAD INTERESTS. SHE WAS A LECTURER, A LABOR LAWYER, A SUFFRAGIST ORGANIZER, ORATOR, A PACIFIST, SOCIALIST, AND WAR CORRESPONDENT (1915). SHE LED A SUFFRAGE MARCH IN WASHINGTON, D.C. IN ROBES ASTRIDE A TALL WHITE HORSE, BEAUTIFUL AND SYMBOLIC. SOME ONLOOKERS JEERED AND ATTACKED THE MARCHERS. OVER 100 MARCHERS WERE INJURED. IN 1916 SHE DIED AT THE AGE OF 30 ON A WESTERN TRIP URGING TO DEFEAT PRESIDENT WILSON FOR NOT ENDORSING SUFFRAGE. HER LAST WORDS WERE, "MR PRESIDENT, HOW LONG MUST WOMEN WAIT FOR LIBERTY." INEZ MILHOLLAND IS BURIED IN LEWIS.

1886
1916

© MARTY PODSKOCH — SAM GLANZMAN 2005

KATE 1907 1986 SMITH

SINGER KATHRYN "KATE" ELIZABETH SMITH, "THE FIRST LADY OF RADIO," HAD A SUMMER COTTAGE "CAMP SUNSHINE," ON AN ISLAND IN LAKE PLACID FOR FORTY YEARS. IN 1926 SHE FIRST PERFORMED ON BROADWAY BUT WAS USED MAINLY FOR COMIC "FAT GIRL" ROLES THAT SHE DESPISED. IN 1930 SHE MET TED COLLINS OF COLUMBIA RECORDS, WHO DEVELOPED HER RADIO SHOW, "KATE SMITH SINGS" (1931-47). HER THEME SONG WAS "WHEN THE MOON COMES OVER THE MOUNTAIN." IN 1938, SHE INTRODUCED IRVING BERLIN'S "GOD BLESS AMERICA" TO THE COUNTRY. KATE MADE OVER 2,000 RECORDINGS — 19 SOLD OVER A MILLION COPIES. IN 1950 SHE BEGAN A FOUR-YEAR TV CAREER WITH "THE KATE SMITH HOUR" AND APPEARED ON OTHER TV SHOWS. IN 1965 KATE WAS BAPTIZED AT A LOCAL CHURCH IN LAKE PLACID AND IN 1986 SHE WAS BURIED IN ST. AGNES CEMETERY IN LAKE, PLACID, NEW YORK.

©2005 MARTY POOSKOCH - SAM GLANZMAN

FIRST AUTO IN ADIRONDACKS

THE FIRST AUTOMOBILE DRIVEN IN THE ADIRONDACKS WAS IN JULY 1902 WHEN HERB SACKETT OF BUFFALO TOOK HIS NEW BRIDE ON THEIR HONEYMOON. THE NEWLYWEDS WORE GOGGLES AND COTTON OVERCOATS, BECAUSE THERE WAS NO WINDSHIELD AND NO ROOF PROTECTION AGAINST THE ELEMENTS AS THEY PUTTED DOWN DUSTY ROADS. THEY SPENT 1 NIGHT AT THE AMPERSAND HOTEL ON LOWER SARANAC LAKE AND THE NEXT DAY SURPRISED THE STAFF AT PAUL SMITHS HOTEL WITH THE NOISE AND CLATTER OF THEIR CONTRAPTION. ALONG THE WAY HORSE-DRAWN CARRIAGES BOLTED AS HERB TOOLED MERRILY ALONG. HISTORIAN AL DONALDSON RECORDED THAT THE "... PUFFING AND POUNDING MOTOR SPREAD TERROR BEFORE IT AND LEFT WRECKAGE AND A-NATHEMA BEHIND IT." NO SERIOUS PROBLEMS OCCURRED, HOWEVER, AND DONALDSON REPORTED THAT THE EVENT WAS MUCH-DISCUSSED BY LOCAL FOLK.

© 2006 - MARTY PODSKOCH - SAM GLANZMAN

VAGABONDS

EDISON · FORD · BURROUGHS · FIRESTONE

"VAGABONDS" IS HOW THOMAS EDISON, HENRY FORD, HARVEY FIRESTONE AND JOHN BURROUGHS DESCRIBED THEMSELVES WHEN THEY TOOK AUTOMOBILE CAMPING TRIPS IN THE ADIRONDACKS AND OTHER SOJURNS THROUGHOUT AMERICA TO GET AWAY FROM THEIR BUSY LIVES. EACH HELPED: EDISON "NAVIGATOR", FORD "MECHANIC," FIRESTONE "ORGANIZER" AND BURROUGHS THE "NATURALIST." A CARAVAN OF CARS AND TRUCKS CARRIED THE "VAGABONDS," WORKERS, A COOK, CAMPING EQUIPMENT AND A CHUCK WAGON. FORD ORGANIZED CONTESTS, SUCH AS SPRINTS, TREE CLIMBING, AND TREE CHOPPING. AFTER DINNER THEY RELAXED BY THE CAMPFIRE DISCUSSING ISSUES OF THE DAY. EACH VAGABOND HAD HIS OWN TENT WITH ELECTRIC LIGHTS. THEY TRAVELED THROUGH THE ADIRONDACKS TWICE. IN 1916 THEY CAMPED NEAR SARATOGA SPRINGS, INDIAN LAKE, ELIZABETHTOWN, AUSABLE FORKS, PAUL SMITHS AND PLATTSBURGH. IN 1919 THEY PICKED THEIR SPOTS AS THE DAY ALLOWED: LOON LAKE, LONG LAKE, LAKE PLACID AND PLATTSBURGH. THEY WERE THE SOURCE OF MANY NEWS STORIES AND THEIR TRIPS LED NYS TO BUILD CAMPSITES TO ENCOURAGE AUTO CAMPING. © 2006 MARTY PODSKOCH — SAM GLANZMAN

VETERANS ☆ MEMORIAL
HIGHWAY ON
WHITEFACE MOUNTAIN

THE VETERANS MEMORIAL HIGHWAY (VMH), AN 8-MILE TWO-LANED PAVED ROAD BUILT DURING THE 1930s TOOK TOURISTS FROM WILMINGTON TO A PARKING LOT BELOW THE SUMMIT OF WHITEFACE MT (4,867'), THE HIGHEST PEAK IN NY. THE COMPLETION OF THE ROAD UP PIKE'S PEAK, COLORADO IN 1918 INSPIRED THE BUILDING OF THE (VMH). MARCELLUS LEONARD, A SARANAC BUSINESSMAN, FOSTERED THE HIGHWAY BUT OPPOSITION HELD THE IDEA UP BECAUSE THE AREA WAS TO BE "FOREVER WILD."
IN 1927 A NYS AMENDMENT ALLOWED CONSTRUCTION, WHICH BEGAN IN DEC. 1931. CREWS STRIPPED THOUSANDS OF TREES AND USED OVER 32 BOXCARS OF DYNAMITE TO CARVE OUT THE ROAD. A MILLION-DOLLAR BOND FINANCED THE PROJECT AND WAS PAID OFF IN TOLLS. ON JULY 20, 1935, PRESIDENT FRANKLIN D. ROOSEVELT OPENED THE HIGHWAY DEDICATING IT TO WWI VETERANS. IN 1936 OVER 100,000 VISITORS ENJOYED THE SUMMIT'S PANORAMIC VIEW. THE ROAD IS OPEN FROM MID-MAY TO EARLY OCTOBER.

© 2006 MARTY PODSKOCH — SAM GLANZMAN

PAUL C. RANSOM

ADIRONDACK-FLORIDA SCHOOL

LADY EMPLOYEES - 1913

IN 1903 PAUL C. RANSOM, LAWYER AND EDUCATOR, FOUNDED THE ADIRONDACK-FLORIDA SCHOOL, THE FIRST MIGRATORY, PRIVATE BOARDING SCHOOL IN THE U.S. IT HAD HIGH STANDARDS AND ENROLLMENT WAS LIMITED TO RICH BOYS. DURING THE SPRING AND FALL, STUDENTS LIVED AND STUDIED AT MEENAGHA (INDIAN FOR BLUE-BERRIES) LODGE CAMPUS ON CLEAR POND NEAR RAINBOW LAKE IN FRANKLIN CO. OLD LOGGING BUILDINGS BECAME CLASSROOMS AND DORMITORIES. CLASSES ENDED AT THANKSGIVING AND RESUMED AT "PINE KNOT CAMP" IN COCONUT GROVE, FLORIDA FOR THE WINTER SESSION THE ADIRONDACK CAMPUS CLOSED IN 1949 BUT THE SCHOOL REMAINED IN COCONUT GROVE, RENAMED RANSOM.
IN 1952 BUSTER CRABBE BOUGHT MEENAGHA AND RAN A SUMMER CAMP UNTIL 1974.

©2004 MARTY PODSKOCH—SAM GLANZMAN

RANGER SCHOOL

MAIN BUILDING FROM AN OLD PHOTO - CIRCA - 1930

© 2005 MARTY PODSKOCH - SAM GLANZMAN

THE NEW YORK STATE RANGER SCHOOL IN WANAKENA NEAR CRANBERRY LAKE HAS TRAINED NEARLY 4,000 MEN AND WOMEN IN FOREST TECHNOLOGY SINCE 1912. J. OTTO HAMELE, THE CHIEF MILLWRIGHT AT THE FORD SAWMILL, HELPED START THE SCHOOL AFTER SEEING THE DAMAGE CAUSED BY CARELESS LOGGING PRACTICES. HE CONVINCED THE RICH LUMBER CO. TO DONATE 1,800 ACRES TO THE NY STATE COLLEGE OF FORESTRY IN SYRACUSE FOR A RANGER SCHOOL. DURING THE SUMMER OF 1912 THE FIRST STUDENTS AND FACULTY CLEARED THE LAND AND BUILT A SMALL SHED THAT SERVED AS BUNKHOUSE, CLASSROOM, KITCHEN, OFFICE, AND DINING ROOM. THE NEXT YEAR A THREE-STORY BUILDING WAS ADDED AND THE FIRST CLASS GRADUATED. IN 1920 SOME OF THE STUDENTS HAD TO LIVE IN TENTS BECAUSE THE ENROLLMENT INCREASED BECAUSE OF WWI VETERANS. IN 1928 A LARGE MAIN BUILDING REPLACED THE SMALLER BUILDINGS. THE SCHOOL ADDED A WEST WING IN 1961 AND IN 2002 THEY EXPANDED THE DORMITORY AND ADDED A LECTURE HALL FOR DISTANCE LEARNING. THE RANGER SCHOOL HAS A NATIONAL REPUTATION FOR EXCELLENCE.

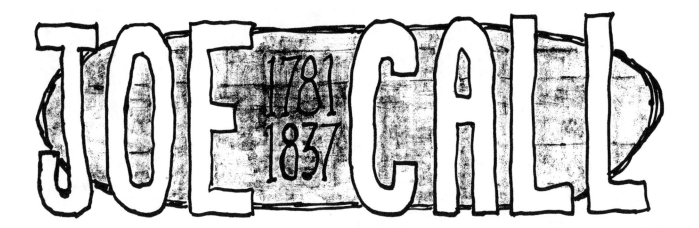

JOE CALL 1781 1837

JOE CALL," THE LEWIS GIANT," REPUTED TO HAVE STRENGTH EQUAL TO THREE MEN, WAS A RENOWNED WRESTLER THROUGHOUT THE CHAMPLAIN VALLEY. CALL LIVED IN LEWIS, ESSEX COUNTY, MARRIED, AND HAD FIVE CHILDREN. HE WAS A FARMER, LOGGER, TEAMSTER, AND A RESPECTED PUBLIC SERVANT. IF HIS WAGON GOT STUCK IN THE MUD HE GOT BENEATH IT AND LIFTED IT OUT. PEOPLE WATCHED IN AWE AT BARN-RAISINGS AS JOE WOULD LIFT MASSIVE TIMBERS BY HIMSELF. DURING THE WAR OF 1812 JOE MET AN ENORMOUS BRITISH SOLDIER, A WRESTLING CHAMPION, WHO DROVE JOE TO HIS KNEES IN A TITANIC LIFE-AND-DEATH STRUGGLE, BUT CALL ROSE, TOOK HIS ENEMY IN A MIGHTY BEAR-HUG AND SQUEEZED HIM UNTIL THE MAN SHRIEKED, QUIVERED, AND WITH EYES BULGING AND BLOOD GUSHING FROM HIS NOSE, FELL DEAD.

© 2005.
MARTY PODSKOCH
SAM GLANZMAN

CLARANCE "BUSTER" CRABBE 1908-1983

NOW * SHOWING

CLARANCE "BUSTER" CRABBE, AN ATHLETE TURNED ACTOR STARRED IN SOME 170 MOVIES. BORN IN OAKLAND, CALIFORNIA HE MOVED TO HAWAII IN 1909. THIS CATAPULTED CRABBE INTO MOVIES STARRING AS: TARZAN, BUCK ROGERS, FLASH GORDON AND CAPTAIN GALLANT. HE ALSO STARRED IN WESTERNS LIKE BILLY THE KID. HE ALSO PROMOTED HIS LINE OF EXERCISE EQUIPMENT AND SWIMMING POOLS. IN 1952 BUSTER PURCHASED THE FLORIDA-ADIRONDACK SCHOOL PROPERTY ON CLEAR POND NEAR RAINBOW LAKE AND THE SARANAC LAKE WHERE HE RAN A BOYS AND GIRLS SUMMER CAMP FOR 23 YEARS.

© MARTY PODSKOCH—SAM GLANZMAN

"GENE"

JAMES
TUNNEY
1897-1978

© 2004 MARTY PODSKOCH - SAM GLANZMAN

JAMES "GENE" TUNNEY, A WORLD CHAMPION BOXER, PUT SPEC-ULATOR ON THE MAP WHEN HE AND OTHERS TRAINED THERE IN THE 1920s AND 1930s. TUNNEY BEGAN HIS PROFESSIONAL BOXING CARRER IN 1915. IN 1922 HE WON THE U.S. LIGHT HEAVYWEIGHT TITLE, BUT FOUR MONTHS LATER LOST IT TO HARRY GREB, HIS ONLY LOSS IN' 77 PROFESSIONAL BOUTS. HE REGAINED THAT TITLE IN 1923. IN 1925 BILL OSBORNE, A WWI MARINE BOXER FRIEND, INVITED TUNNEY TO SPECULATOR TO TRAIN AT THE OSBORNE HOTEL. TUNNEY LIKED THE NATURAL SURROUNDINGS. IN 1926 HE DEFEATED THE WORLD HEAVYWEIGHT CHAMPION, JACK DEMPSEY. HE BEAT HIM AGAIN IN 1927 IN THE "LONG COUNT 10-ROUND FIGHT." TUNNEY RETIRED FROM BOXING IN 1928 AND BECAME A SUCCESSFUL BUSINESSMAN.

MAXIMILIAN ADALBERT "MAX" BAER

1909-1959

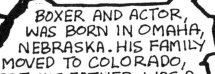

BOXER AND ACTOR, WAS BORN IN OMAHA, NEBRASKA. HIS FAMILY MOVED TO COLORADO, WHERE HIS FATHER WAS A BUTCHER, AND THEN TO CALIFORNIA IN 1921 WHERE HIS FATHER WAS A RANCHER. MAX WAS TERRIFICALLY STRONG AFTER YEARS OF HEAVY WORK WITH HIS FATHER. HE BECAME A PROFESSIONAL BOXER IN 1929. HE BEAT MAX SCHMELING IN 1933 AND PRIMO CARNERA IN 1934 TO BECOME WORLD HEAVY-WEIGHT CHAMPION. DURING THE SUMMER OF 1935 MAX TRAINED IN SPECULATOR FOR HIS FIGHT WITH JOE LOUIS. BAER WAS KO'D IN THE FOURTH ROUND. BAER'S BOX-ING RECORD WAS 72-12 (53 KNOCKOUTS).

BAER ALSO ACTED IN ALMOST TWENTY MOVIES, INCLUDING "THE PRIZEFIGHTER AND THE LADY" AND MADE SEVERAL TV APPEARANCES. BAER'S SON, MAX JR., PLAYED THE ROLE OF JETHRO BODINE IN "THE BEVERLY HILLBILLIES."

1933 BAER KO'S MAX

MAX SCHMELING

1934 BAER KO'S PRIMO

PRIMO CARNERA

FOURTH ROUND JOE LOUIS KO'S MAX

© MARTY PODSKOCH 2004
SAM GLANZMAN

1932 WINTER OLYMPIC GAMES in LAKE PLACID

THE OLYMPIC WINTER GAMES FIRST CAME TO THE U.S. IN 1932 AND WERE HELD IN LAKE PLACID. MELVILLE DEWEY'S SON, GODFREY, HELPED RAISE OVER $1,000,000 TO BUILD AN INDOOR SKATING RINK, A 401-METER BOBSLED RUN, A STADIUM AND TO IMPROVE CROSS-COUNTRY SKI TRAILS, SKI JUMPS, AND THE SPEED-SKATING OVAL. GOV. FRANKLIN D. ROOSEVELT OPENED THE EVENTS. HIS WIFE, ELEANOR, RODE THE BOBSLED RUN. MORE THAN 80,000 ATTENDED. MISHAPS INCLUDED CROSS-COUNTRY SKIERS GETTING LOST, BOBSLED CRASHES, AND BARE SPOTS DUE TO WARM WEATHER. TRUCKS TRANSPORTED IN SNOW FROM VARIOUS SITES. THE 4-MAN BOBSLED COMPETITION ENDED 2 DAYS AFTER THE CLOSING CEREMONIES. THE U.S. WON THE MOST MEDALS--12--INCLUDING GOLD IN ALL 4 SPEED SKATING EVENTS AND IN BOTH BOBSLED EVENTS.

© 2006 - MARTY PODSKOCH - SAM GLANZMAN

JACK SHEA

JACK SHEA WON 2-GOLD MEDALS AT THE 1932 OLYMIC WINTER GAMES IN LAKE PLACID, HIS HOME TOWN. IN HIS FIRST RACE AT 7 YEARS OLD, HE FELL 15' FROM THE START. POLICE CHIEF TOM BLACK PICKED HIM UP AND TOLD HIM THERE WOULD BE OTHER RACES. AT 22, JACK WON THE OLYMPIC 500-METER AND THE 1,500-METER SPEED SKATING RACES IN HIS HOME TOWN. SHEA DID NOT GO TO THE 1936 OLYMPICS IN GERMANY IN PROTEST OF HITLER'S ANTI-SEMITISM. JACK HELPED PERSUADE THE INTERNATIONAL OLYMPIC COMMITTEE TO STAGE THE 1980 WINTER GAMES IN LAKE PLACID. JACK'S FAMILY HAD THREE GENERATIONS OF WINTER OLYMPIANS. HIS SON, JIM, PARTICIPATED IN NORDIC COMBINED AT THE 1964 WINTER GAMES. JACK SHEA DIED IN A CAR ACCIDENT A MONTH BEFORE HIS GRANDSON, JIM JR., WON AN OLYMPIC GOLD MEDAL IN THE 2002 SKELETON EVENT IN SALT LAKE CITY.

© 2006 - MARTY POOSKOCH
SAM GLANZMAN

JACK SHEA

1980 WINTER OLYMPICS

USA LAKE PLACID 1980

ERIC HEIDEN

HERB BROOKS

THE OLYMPIC WINTER GAMES WERE HELD IN LAKE PLACID FOR THE SECOND TIME IN 1980, WHEN 232 WOMEN AND 840 MEN FROM 37 COUNTRIES PARTICIPATED. ALTHOUGH THE U.S. CAME IN THIRD PLACE IN MEDALS BEHIND RUSSIA AND EAST GERMANY, AMERICANS TRIUMPHED IN SPEED SKATING AND HOCKEY. ERIC HEIDEN WAS THE FIRST INDIVIDUAL TO WIN 5 GOLD MEDALS. HE DOMINATED SPEED SKATING WINNING RACES FROM 500 M TO 10,000 M. IN FRONT OF A BOISTEROUS, FLAG-WAVING HOME CROWD, THE U.S. ICE HOCKEY TEAM, COACHED BY HERB BROOKS AND MADE UP PRIMARILY OF COLLEGIATE PLAYERS, SURPRISED THE WORLD WHEN IT DEFEATED THE SUPPOSEDLY INVINCIBLE SOVIET TEAM 4-3 IN A SEMI-FINAL MATCH. THE NEXT DAY WHEN THE U.S. DEFEATED FINLAND FOR THE GOLD MEDAL IT WAS DUBBED "THE MIRACLE ON ICE."

© 2005 - MARTY POOSKOCH - SAM GLANZMAN

"SNOW TRAINS" BROUGHT WINTER SPORT ENTHUSIASTS TO THE ADIRONDACKS IN THE EARLY 1930s AFTER MANY WERE INSPIRED BY THE 1932 WINTER OLYMPICS IN LAKE PLACID. PEOPLE WHO WERE HEADED FOR HOTELS NEAR OLD FORGE RODE THE NY CENTRAL FROM NYC AND WESTERN NY TO THE THENDARA STATION. NORTH CREEK, IN THE SOUTHEASTERN ADIRONDACKS, WAS ANOTHER DESTINATION FOR SKIERS. ON MARCH 4, 1934 THE FIRST SNOW TRAIN LEFT NYC AT 12:45 A.M. AND ARRIVED AT NORTH CREEK AT 7:20 A.M. WITH 378 PASSENGERS INCLUDING SOME FROM SCHENECTADY. SAKS 5TH AVENUE PROVIDED A RAILROAD CAR WITH SKI RENTALS AND EQUIPMENT. SKIERS RODE UP MOUNTAINS IN OPEN TRUCKS, BUSES AND CARS AND SLID DOWN. AFTER TWO DAYS OF SKIING PASSENGERS RETURNED TO GRAND CENTRAL STATION AT 11:05 PM. THE ERA OF THE SNOW TRAIN ENDED AROUND 1940.

© 2007 MARTY PODSKOCH - SAM GLANZMAN

ADIRONDACK BATS

SINCE 1946," ADIRONDACK "BATS,
MADE IN THE SOUTHERN EDGE OF
THE ADIRONDACKS IN DOLGEVILLE,
HAVE BEEN USED BY MANY MAJOR
LEAGUE BASEBALL PLAYERS IN-
CLUDING MEL OTT, WILLIE MAYS,
REGGIE JACKSON, STAN MUSIAL,
AND MIKE SCHMIDT. A FORMER
NY GIANT PITCHER FROM CAN-
ADA LAKE, HAL SCHUMACHER,
WORKED AS A SALESMAN AND
CONVINCED BIG LEAGUE PLAY-
ERS TO USE THE "ADIRONDACK"
BATS. MADE FROM NORTHERN
WHITE ASH LOGS THAT ARE CUT
INTO 40" LENGTHS, HAND-SPLIT
INTO 6 OR 8 PIECES, KILN-DRIED,
ROUNDED ON LATHES, SANDED,
COLORED AND FINISHED WITH A
CLEAR LACQUER OR PAINTED RED,
BLACK OR A TWO-TONED. HARD
MAPLE BATS ARE NOW BECOMING
POPULAR AND ACCOUNT FOR ABOUT
40% OF SALES. EACH YEAR
ABOUT 400,000 BATS ARE PRO-
DUCED BY RAWLINGS SPORTING
GOODS CO., A DIVISION OF K2 INC.

MEL OTT

Adirondack

© MARTY PODSKOCH – SAM GLANZMAN – 2005

JOHNNY PODRES

JOHNNY PODRES, NOTED BASEBALL PITCHER FOR THE BROOKLYN DODGERS, WAS BORN IN 1932 IN WITHERBEE NEAR PORT HENRY. HIS FATHER WORKED IN AN UNDERGROUND IRON-ORE MINE. JOHNNY THE ELDEST OF FIVE CHILDREN, ENJOYED HUNTING AND FISHING. HE WAS AN OUTSTANDING PITCHER FOR MINEVILLE HIGH SCHOOL, AT THE TIME ATTRACTING A BROOKLYN DODGERS SCOUT. IN 1951 HE PLAYED IN THE MINORS AND IN 1953 WAS CALLED UP TO THE DODGERS. IN THE 1955 WORLD SERIES PODRES BEAT THE YANKEES IN GAME 3 AND SHUT THEM OUT 2-0 IN GAME 7, GIVING BROOKLYN ITS ONLY SERIES TITLE AFTER FIVE CONSECUTIVE LOSSES TO THEIR BRONX RIVALS. AFTER A SUCCESSFUL 16-YEAR CAREER IN THE MAJORS HE RETIRED AND WAS A PITCHING COACH. TODAY HE DIVIDES HIS TIME BETWEEN QUEENSBURY AND WITHERBEE. HE STILL ENJOYS FISHING IN THE ADIRONDACKS.

SARANAC LAKE WINTER CARNIVAL

THE SARANAC LAKE CARNIVAL, THE OLDEST WINTER FESTIVAL IN THE EASTERN UNITED STATES, BEGAN IN 1897 WHEN THE PONTIAC CLUB CREATED ENTERTAINMENT FOR THE TUBERCULOSIS PATIENTS WHO CAME TO SARANAC LAKE TO 'TAKE THE CURE'. A TWO-DAY WINTER CARNIVAL DREW PATIENTS OUTSIDE INTO THE FRESH AIR AND MILES OF FROZEN LAKES AND TRAILS. THERE WERE SKATING RACES, HARNESS RACES ON ICE, A PARADE, AND A FANCY COSTUME BALL. ONE YEAR AN ARCHITECT RECOVERING FROM TB HELPED ADD AN 'ICE FORTRESS'. EACH YEAR THE 'ICE PALACE' BECAME MORE ELABORATE WITH TOWERS, TURRETS, TORCHES, FIREWORKS, AND LATER COLORED ELECTRIC LIGHTS. ABOUT 1,500 BLOCKS OF ICE (3-500 LBS) CUT FROM LAKE FLOWER FORM A CASTLE SOME 80¹ LONG AND 50¹ HIGH. HELD IN EARLY FEBRUARY, THE WINTER CARNIVAL INCLUDES RACES, CONCERTS, SNOW SCULPTURES, DINNERS, DANCES, AND THE CROWNING OF ROYALTY.

PROSPECT MOUNTAIN INCLINE RAILWAY

PROSPECT MT. HOUSE

INCLINE RAILWAY

BULLWHEEL

THE PROSPECT MOUNTAIN INCLINED RAILWAY (1895-1903) WAS BUILT BY OWNERS OF THE PROSPECT MOUNTAIN HOUSE TO ATTRACT TOURISTS TO THEIR HOTEL AT THE SUMMIT. PEOPLE ARRIVED ON THE DELAWARE AND HUDSON RR IN CALDWELL (LAKE GEORGE) AND PAID 50 CENTS FOR THE ROUND TRIP TICKET. THEY BOARDED AN OPEN SIDED CAR THAT WAS PULLED UP BY A 7,150' CABLE ATTACHED TO THE FRONT OF THE CAR FROM AN ENGINE AT THE SUMMIT POWERHOUSE. ANOTHER CAR ATTACHED TO THE CABLE AT THE TOP, CAME DOWN AT THE SAME TIME. THE CARS MET AT A TURN-OUT HALFWAY AND PASSED EACH OTHER. AT THE SUMMIT TOURISTS HAD A PANORAMIC VIEW OF LAKE GEORGE AND PEAKS IN 4 STATES. BY 1904, THE RAILWAY WAS SHUT DOWN AND IT LAY IDLE UNTIL WWI, WHEN IT WAS USED FOR SCRAP. A HUGE WHEEL LEFT AT THE SUMMIT IS THE ONLY REMINDER OF THE ONCE POPULAR RAILWAY.

© 2006 — MARTY RODSKOCH — SAM GLANZMAN

SANTA'S WORKSHOP

JULIAN REISS OF LAKE PLACID TOLD HIS YOUNG DAUGHTER ABOUT A BABY BEAR WHO DISCOVERED SANTA CLAUS AND HIS NORTH POLE WORKSHOP. SHE PLEADED TO VISIT THIS MAGICAL PLACE, SO JULIAN BUILT SANTA'S 'SUMMER HOME.' ARTO MONACO OF UPPER JAY, A FORMER DISNEY CARTOONIST, DESIGNED 'SANTA'S WORKSHOP' ON 14 ACRES IN WILMINGTON. IT OPENED JULY 1, 1949 AND WAS THE FIRST US THEME PARK WITH A 'NORTH POLE,' A SANTA'S HOUSE AND WORKSHOP WITH ITS OWN POST OFFICE, A CHILDREN'S VILLAGE OF BRIGHTLY PAINTED LOG HOUSES, KIDDIE RIDES, AN ARCADE, MUSICAL SHOWS, AND GIFT SHOPS. IN ITS EARLY DAYS UP TO 10,000 SUMMERTIME TOURISTS A DAY VISITED. IT WAS THE WORLD'S FIRST PETTING ZOO WITH GOATS, SHEEP AND DEER WANDERING ABOUT. THE ANIMALS ARE GONE BECAUSE THEY NIBBLED THE TOURIST'S CLOTHES. REINDEER PULL SANTA'S SLEIGH, AND COSTUMED CHARACTERS, INCLUDING FROSTY THE SNOWMAN, LEAD THE AFTERNOON CHRISTMAS PARADE AND DANCE WITH THE CHILDREN.

© 2005 MARTY POOSKOCH - SAM GLANZMAN

ARTO MONACO'S LAND OF MAKEBELIEVE

LAND OF MAKEBELIEVE

The Land of Makebelieve designed with wonderous Things for Kids to see So, Mom, Dad sit down relax and Let the Kids w___ free

ARTO MONACO (1913-2003), ONCE A CARTOONIST FOR WALT DISNEY, DESIGNED AND BUILT SEVERAL THEME PARKS IN THE AD-IRONDACKS. IN 1949 HE CREATED "SANTA'S WORK-SHOP" IN WILMINGTON AND THEN OLD McDONALD'S FARM NEAR LAKE PLACID FOR JULIAN REISS. AFTER BUILDING HUNDREDS OF SMALL -SCALE BUILDINGS FOR DISPLAY, HE BUILT HIS OWN CHILD-SIZED PARK: THE LAND OF MAKEBELIEVE, ALONG THE AUSABLE RIVER IN UPPER JAY. IT OPENED IN THE SUMMER OF 1954. HE BUILT A THREE-STORY CAS-TLE WHERE KIDS COULD BE KING OR QUEEN FOR A DAY. THERE WAS A RIVER BOAT, A TRAIN, A STAGECOACH, FAIRYTALE HOUSES, AN OLD WESTERN TOWN, AND CARS THAT KIDS COULD DRIVE AROUND THE PARK. THEY ALSO RODE ON A FIRE TRUCK, STEAMBOATS AND EVEN A HORSE-DRAWN STAGECOACH. ARTO SAID: "KIDS COULD DO WHATEVER THEY WANTED, AND YOU COULDN'T BOTHER THEM." THERE WAS ALSO A PETTING ZOO. LOCAL KIDS HAD A SECRET ENTRANCE AND GOT IN FOR FREE. THEY CALLED HIM "UNCLE ARTO." THE PARK CLOSED IN 1979 AFTER A DEVASTATING FLOOD.

© 2006 MARTY POUSKOSH - SAM GLANZMAN

FRONTIER TOWN, A 267-ACRE OLD WEST-THEME PARK NEAR THE NORTHWAY IN NORTH HUDSON FROM 1951 TO 1985, WAS CREATED BY ART BENSON, A STATEN ISLAND TELEPHONE INSTALLER, SO THAT FAMILIES COULD TAKE A "STEP BACK IN HISTORY." FOR MANY YEARS ART EXPLORED THE NORTHEAST SEARCHING FOR LAND TO BUILD HIS PARK. HE FINALLY FOUND A 100-ACRE FARM ALONG SCHROON RIVER AND PAID $1,800 FROM A MAYONNAISE JAR UNDER HIS CAR SEAT. THE NEXT DAY BENSON HIRED FIVE WORKERS TO BEGIN CUTTING TREES AND MAKING LOG STRUCTURES FOR A BLOCKHOUSE, CHURCH, SCHOOLHOUSE, STABLE, CRAFT SHOPS, CANTEEN, TRADING POST AND A HOME. TO STAFF THE AUTHENTIC VILLAGE, THERE WAS A BLACKSMITH, A GLASS BLOWER, WEAVERS, AND A SILVERSMITH. FOR HIS WILD-WEST SHOWS LOCAL FOLK PLAYED INDIANS, COWBOYS, AND SOLDIERS. FOR OVER 30 YEARS THOUSANDS ENJOYED RODEOS AND RODE REAL STAGECOACHES THAT WERE ROBBED. KIDS BECAME DEPUTIES AND SAW THE THIEVES BROUGHT TO JUSTICE IN THE "DUNKIN POOL." IT HAD A MOTEL, RESTAURANT AND AIRPORT. IN 1985 ART CLOSED THE PARK DUE TO ILL HEALTH.

ART BENSON

©2006 MIKEY POPSKITCH

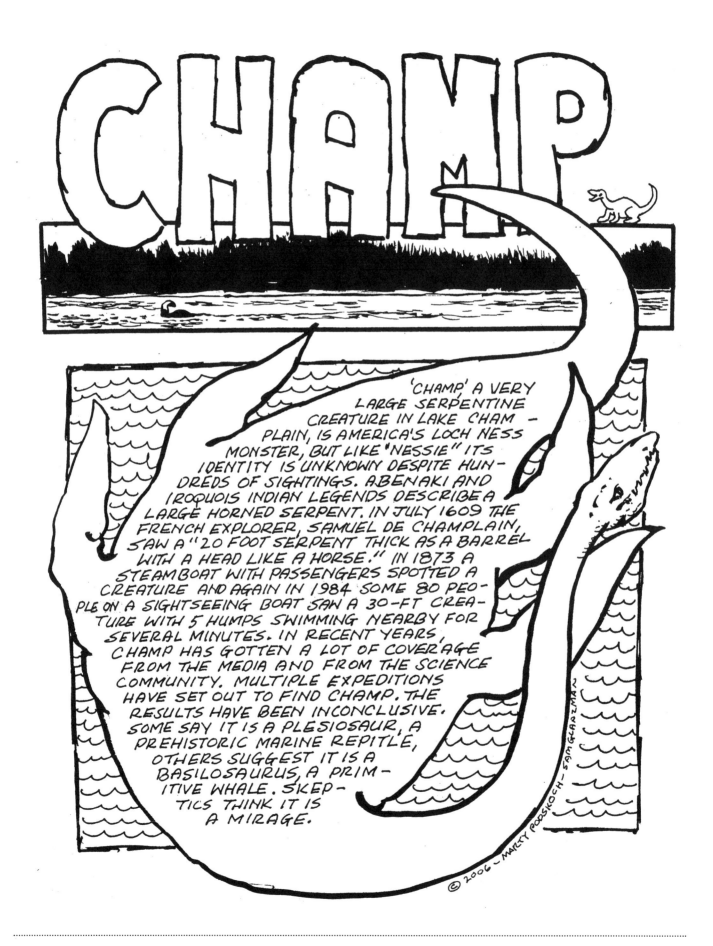

CHAMP

'CHAMP' A VERY LARGE SERPENTINE CREATURE IN LAKE CHAMPLAIN, IS AMERICA'S LOCH NESS MONSTER, BUT LIKE "NESSIE" ITS IDENTITY IS UNKNOWN DESPITE HUNDREDS OF SIGHTINGS. ABENAKI AND IROQUOIS INDIAN LEGENDS DESCRIBE A LARGE HORNED SERPENT. IN JULY 1609 THE FRENCH EXPLORER, SAMUEL DE CHAMPLAIN, SAW A "20 FOOT SERPENT THICK AS A BARREL WITH A HEAD LIKE A HORSE." IN 1873 A STEAMBOAT WITH PASSENGERS SPOTTED A CREATURE AND AGAIN IN 1984 SOME 80 PEOPLE ON A SIGHTSEEING BOAT SAW A 30-FT CREATURE WITH 5 HUMPS SWIMMING NEARBY FOR SEVERAL MINUTES. IN RECENT YEARS, CHAMP HAS GOTTEN A LOT OF COVERAGE FROM THE MEDIA AND FROM THE SCIENCE COMMUNITY. MULTIPLE EXPEDITIONS HAVE SET OUT TO FIND CHAMP. THE RESULTS HAVE BEEN INCONCLUSIVE. SOME SAY IT IS A PLESIOSAUR, A PREHISTORIC MARINE REPITLE, OTHERS SUGGEST IT IS A BASILOSAURUS, A PRIMITIVE WHALE. SKEPTICS THINK IT IS A MIRAGE.

© 2006 – MARTY PODSKOCH – SAM GLANZMAN

BIG FOOT IN INDIAN LAKE

A SHAGGY HERMIT, KNOWN AS 'BIG FOOT, OR WILDMAN,' ABOUT SIX FEET TALL AND WRAPPED IN ANIMAL SKINS AND RAGS, WAS SEEN MANY TIMES AROUND INDIAN LAKE IN THE WINTER OF 1932. IN EARLY FEBRUARY, TWO STATE TROOPERS AT THEIR CAMP NEAR BLUE MT. LAKE SAW A VERY STRANGE FIGURE DISAPPEAR IN THE FALLING SNOW, LEAVING LARGE FOOTPRINTS. RESIDENTS IN THE FULTON CHAIN AREA SAW THIS 'BIG FOOT' WHO LEFT FOOTPRINTS ABOUT 2' AROUND. AFTER REPORTS OF VANDALISM TO CAMPS, PEOPLE BECAME WARY. IN EARLY MARCH, TROOPERS FOUND HIS PRINTS GOING INTO A SAWMILL AND CALLED FOR HIM TO COME OUT. HIS ANSWER,

"LEAVE ME ALONE," FOLLOWED BY GUNFIRE LED TO A SHOOTOUT. A MEMBER OF THE SEARCH PARTY WAS SHOT BUT THE BULLET RICOCHETED OFF A SILVER DOLLAR IN HIS POCKET. WHEN THE POLICE WENT IN THEY FOUND A MAN, IN HIS LATE 20s, DEAD FROM A STOMACH WOUND. HE WAS NEVER IDENTIFIED AND WAS BURIED NEAR NORTH CREEK.

© MARTY PODSKOCH - SAM GLANZMAN 2006

BIG FOOT

BIG FOOT WAS SEEN ON HURRICANE MT. BY FIRE TOWER OBSERVER HANK McCOY ON A SUMMER NIGHT IN 1949. HANK WAS WALKING NEAR HIS FIRE OBSERVER'S CABIN WHEN HE SAW A HUGE MAN-LIKE CREATURE COMING TOWARDS HIM. HE RAN TO GET HIS .22 RIFLE, BUT WHEN HE STEPPED OUT AND SAW THIS HAIRY GIANT ABOUT 20' AWAY HE KNEW HIS GUN WAS USELESS. HANK LOCKED THE DOOR AND HE AND FLORENCE LIFTED THEIR 5 CHILDREN INTO THE LOFT IN THE BEDROOM WHERE THEY WOULD BE SAFE, HOPEFULLY. THE HAIRY GIANT SHOOK THE WHOLE CABIN TERRIFYING THE McCOYS. WHEN THE SHAKING STOPPED, THE PARENTS LOOKED OUT THE WINDOW AND SAW THE MAN-LIKE CREATURE MOVING AWAY AND HEARD HARSH HEAVY SOUNDS. YEARS LATER THE FAMILY SAW TV SHOWS ABOUT BIG FOOT AND WHEN THEY SAW PICTURES AND HEARD THE HARSH SOUNDS, THEY KNEW THEY HAD SEEN HIM ON HURRICANE MT.

© 2006 MARTY POPSUCH – SAM GLADMAN

CLINTON PRISON OR "LITTLE SIBERIA," IS THE LARGEST AND THIRD OLDEST PRISON IN NY. IT WAS BEGUN IN 1845 TO USE CONVICTS TO MINE AND MANUFACTURE IRON. RANSOM COOK OF SARATOGA SURVEYED THE AREA AND CHOOSE A 200-ACRE PARCEL IN DANNEMORA, 17 MILES WEST OF PLATTSBURGH. COOK, THE FIRST WARDEN, HAD WORKERS CLEAR THE LAND AND BUILT A STOCKADE AND TEMPORARY BUILDINGS FOR OFFICERS, GUARDS, WORKMEN AND CONVICTS. HE WENT TO SING SING AND AUBURN PRISONS AND SELECTED 50 STRONG AND HEALTHY CONVICTS WHO WERE TRANSPORTED TO PLATTSBURGH AND THEN THEY WALKED THE TREACHEROUS AND STEEP TRAIL IN SHACKLES, ANKLE-CHAINS, AND STRIPES. THE BEDRAGGLED MEN ARRIVED ON JUNE 3, 1845. THE PRISONERS CONSTRUCTED A KITCHEN, BLACKSMITH SHOP, STEAM SAWMILL, ORE BUILDINGS, AND AN IRON AND BRASS FOUNDRY. COOK TREATED HIS PRISONERS WITH KINDNESS AND EVEN DISPENSED WITH SHACKLES AND CHAINS DURING WORK.

EARLY CLINTON PRISON — DANNEMORA —

RANSOM COOK

©2005 MARTY PODSKOCH - SAM GLANZMAN

STAGECOACH ROBBERY

ON THE AFTERNOON OF AUGUST 14th 1901, A LONE GUNMAN ROBBED A BLUE MOUNTAIN STAGECOACH ON ITS WAY FROM NORTH CREEK TO INDIAN LAKE. THERE WERE 7 PASSENGERS: 3 MEN ON TOP WITH THE DRIVER, WILL ELDRIDGE, AND 3 WOMEN AND A MAN INSIDE THE COACH. AS THE COACH NEARED THE TOP OF COON HILL A MASKED MAN STEPPED OUT AND ORDERED THE DRIVER TO HALT. WILL FLUNG THE MAILBAGS TO THE SIDE AND CONTINUED RIGHT AT THE BANDIT, WHO THEN SHOT A LEAD HORSE, WHICH PULLED THE HORSES DOWN. THREE MEN RAN INTO THE WOODS BUT WILL REMAINED. EDWARD BERNSTEIN WHO WAS RIDING SHOTGUN HEARD BULLETS WHISTLING BY HIS HEAD AS HE RAN INTO THE WOODS BUT HE WAS DETERMINED TO PROTECT THE $7,000 IN HIS POCKET. THE GUNMAN ONLY GOT $20 FROM A PASSENGER. HE FLED ON HEARING ANOTHER WAGON, DRIVEN BY JACK CARR APPROACHING. CARR LOANED WILL A HORSE AND THE COACH RETURNED TO NORTH CREEK. AFTER HIDING FOR AN HOUR BERNSTEIN RETURNED TO FIND THE STAGE GONE. HE CRAWLED 6 MILES TO INDIAN LAKE WITH AN INJURED ANKLE AND HIS CASH. THE THIEF WAS NEVER CAUGHT.

© 2006 - MARTY PODSKOCH - SAM GLANZMAN

UNSOLVED MURDER

ORRANDO P. DEXTER (D.1903) WAS A CAN-
TANKEROUS MILLIONAIRE LAWYER WITH A
7,000-ACRE ESTATE ABOUT 5 MILES SOUTH
OF ST. REGIS FALLS FOR SOME 15 YEARS
OF SUMMERS AND VACATIONS. DEXTER WAS
ROYALLY UNPOPULAR WITH LOCAL FOLK BE-
CAUSE HE WAS ALWAYS SUING SOMEBODY
AND HE SECLUDED HIMSELF BEHIND FENCES
WITH SECURITY GUARDS. ON SATURDAY
AFTERNOON SEPTEMBER 9, 1903, DEXTER
HAD JUST LEFT HIS HOME AND WAS
DRIVING HIS BUGGY TO SANTA CLARA,
WHEN A RIFLEMAN STEPPED OUT AFTER
HE PASSED, AND SHOT HIM IN THE BACK. THE
BULLET PASSED THROUGH HIM AND INTO
HIS HORSE'S RUMP. THE ANIMAL BOLTED
THROWING DEXTER TO THE GROUND, DEAD.
   EVEN THOUGH IT IS LIKELY PEOPLE KNEW
WHO THE CULPRIT WAS, NO ONE WAS EVER
CAUGHT DESPITE A #5,000 REWARD AND
CLOSE SCRUTINY BY LOCAL POLICE AND BIG
CITY DETECTIVES.

GILLETTE MURDER

1906

H FORMER TO LYNC GILLETTE!

CHESTER GILLETTE

GRACE BROWN

GEORGE W. WARD
DISTRICT ATTORNEY

IRVING DEVENDORF
JUDGE

© MARTY PODSKOCH — SAM GLANZMAN

MURDER IN THE ADIRONDACKS ...

THE ADIRONDACK'S BIG MOOSE LAKE WAS THE SETTING FOR A MURDER CASE IN-VOLVING CHESTER GILLETTE, A YOUNG MAN ACCUSED OF KILLING GRACE BROWN. THE TWO HAD MET AT A FACTORY IN CORTLAND, N.Y. AFTER SECRETLY DATING, GRACE BECAME PREGNANT. CHESTER TOOK HER BOATING KNOWING THAT SHE COULDN'T SWIM. HER DEAD BODY WAS FOUND IN THE LAKE WITH A BLOW TO THE HEAD. CHESTER WAS ARRESTED AND EVENTUALLY CONVICTED OF THE MURDER. HE DIED IN THE ELECTRIC CHAIR.
.... THEODORE DREISER'S BOOK, AN AMERICAN TRAGEDY (1925) AND THE MOVIES: AN AMERICAN TRAGEDY (1931) AND A PLACE IN THE SUN ARE BASED ON THIS 1906 MURDER.

TROOP B'S
BLACK HORSE
BRIGADE

THE BLACK HORSE BRIGADE WAS NY STATE POLICE TROOP B ESTABLISHED IN 1921 TO COVER THE NORTHERN ADIRONDACKS AND THE CANADIAN BORDER. IT WAS ALSO CALLED GRAY RIDERS AND THE BROADFIELD BOYS, WITH HEADQUARTERS IN MALONE UNDER CAPTAIN C.J. BROADFIELD. THE 56 TROOPERS WERE REQUIRED TO EXPERTLY SWIM, DIVE, RIDE A HORSE, DRIVE AN AUTO, AND GO ANYWHERE TO CATCH THEIR MAN. ON DUTY 24-HOURS, THEY WERE ARMED WITH A COLT .45 AND A WINCHESTER RIFLE FOR $950 A YEAR. WITH 50 BLACK HORSES, 2-MAN TEAMS PATROLLED 2-WEEK SHIFTS AVERAGING 20-40 MILES A DAY WHILE KEEPING IN CONTACT BY PHONE OR POST-CARD. TROOP B HAD TWO OR MORE TROOPERS IN 12 ZONE STATIONS IN LAKE PLACID, ELIZABETHTOWN, PORT HENRY, SCHROON LAKE, STAR LAKE, TUPPER LAKE, LOWVILLE, CANTON, GOUVERNEUR, MASSENA, CLAYTON, AND ROUSES POINT. DURING PROHIBITION (1920-1933), TROOP B TRIED TO STOP ALCOHOL FROM CROSSING THE CANADIAN BORDER. TROOP B USED 50 HORSES TILL 1932.

RUMRUNNERS
IN THE
ADIRONDACKS

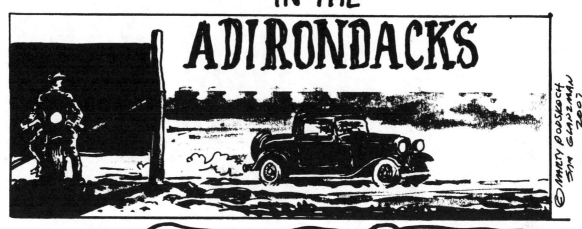

© MARTY PODSKOCH
JIM GLANZMAN
2007

DURING PROHIBITION (1920-32) DAREDEVIL RUMRUNNERS IN THE ADIRONDACKS CARRIED BEER, RAW ALCOHOL AND WHISKEY FROM CANADA IN HORSE-DRAWN SLEIGHS WHEN NECESSARY BUT MOSTLY IN "SOUPED UP" CARS. BIG SEDANS LIKE PACKARDS AND CADILLACS COULD CARRY 33 CASES OF ALE. THEIR BAG OF TRICKS INCLUDED LICENSE PLATES THAT CHANGED, TANKS THAT SPILLED OIL BEHIND, OR BLINDING SMOKE SCREENS. ONE BOOTLEGGER INSTALLED FALSE PARTITIONS THAT HID 1,000 BOTTLES OF BEER, 12 BOTTLES OF WHISKEY AND 19 QUARTS OF WINE. ROUTE 30 THROUGH MALONE AND ROUTE 9 WERE FAVORITE ROUTES. MOST TRAVELED UNDER COVER OF DARKNESS TO AVOID THE BORDER PATROL AND STATE POLICE. DRIVERS WERE VERY SKILLFUL AT HIGH SPEEDS AND COULD DO A 180 AND PASS THEIR PURSUERS. "RATTERS" WHO TOLD THE AUTHORITIES ABOUT CAPERS WERE DEALT WITH HARSHLY. HIJACKERS TOOK THEIR SHARE OF THE CONTRABAND. THERE WERE GUN BATTLES KILLING AND INJURING BOTH POLICE AND RUMRUNNERS. RUMRUNNING ENDED IN 1933 WITH THE REPEAL OF PROHIBITION.

GREAT WINDFALL 1845

ON SEPTEMBER 20, 1845 A MONSTER TORNADO SWEPT ACROSS THE NORTHERN PART OF THE ADIRONDACKS TO LAKE CHAMPLAIN LEAVING THE LARGEST RECORDED PATH OF DESTRUCTION IN THE STATE. IT CAME FROM LAKE ONTARIO, HEADED EAST, AND CROSSED THE OSWEGATCHIE RIVER NEAR CRANBERRY LAKE. WHEN IT TOUCHED DOWN IT LIFTED A SCHOOLHOUSE FROM ITS FOUNDATION. LUCKILY, NO ONE WAS HURT. THE TWISTER SPLIT NEAR THE FRANKLIN COUNTY LINE AND CREATED TWO PARALLEL MILE-WIDE PATHS OF SNAPPED OFF AND UPROOTED TREES. EGG-SIZED HAILSTONES FOLLOWED AND SERIOUSLY IN- JURED CATTLE. THE TWISTED PILE OF TREES WAS IMPENETRABLE, SO HUNTERS SET PARTS OF THE SLASH AFIRE TO RE-OPEN THEIR TRAILS. EVENTUALLY A BROAD BAND OF GRASS REPLACED THE TREES AND YEARS LATER IT WAS PRETTY WELL COVERED BY SECOND-GROWTH TIMBER. TWO PONDS, TWO BROOKS, AND A LOCAL RESTAURANT ARE NAMED WINDFALL.

© 2005 MARTY PODSKOCH - SAM GLANZMAN

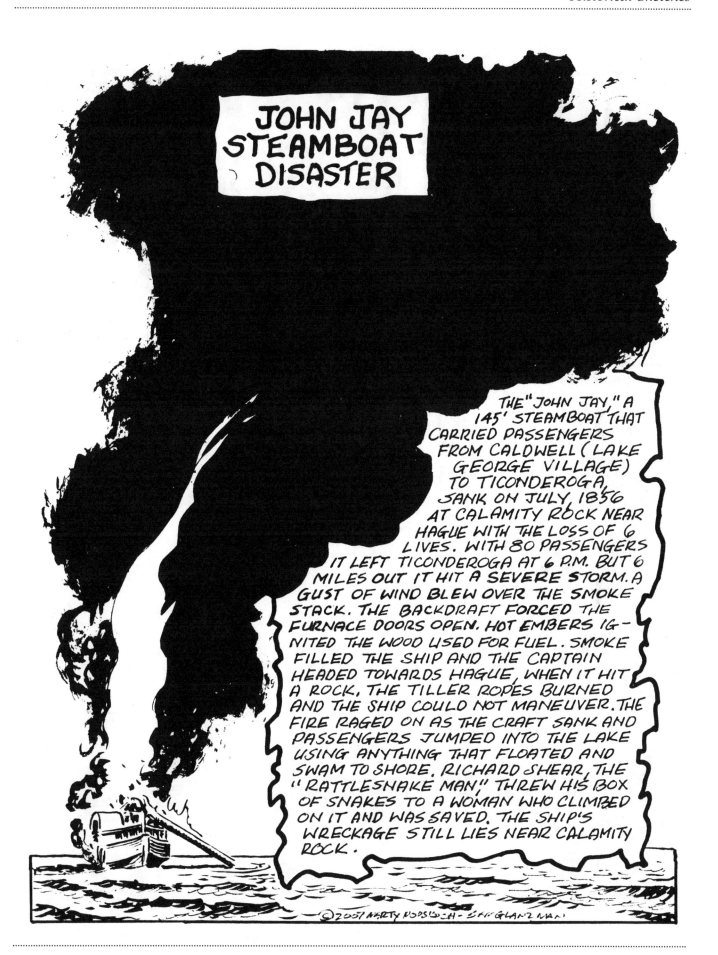

JOHN JAY STEAMBOAT DISASTER

THE "JOHN JAY," A 145' STEAMBOAT THAT CARRIED PASSENGERS FROM CALDWELL (LAKE GEORGE VILLAGE) TO TICONDEROGA, SANK ON JULY, 1856 AT CALAMITY ROCK NEAR HAGUE WITH THE LOSS OF 6 LIVES. WITH 80 PASSENGERS IT LEFT TICONDEROGA AT 6 P.M. BUT 6 MILES OUT IT HIT A SEVERE STORM. A GUST OF WIND BLEW OVER THE SMOKE STACK. THE BACKDRAFT FORCED THE FURNACE DOORS OPEN. HOT EMBERS IGNITED THE WOOD USED FOR FUEL. SMOKE FILLED THE SHIP AND THE CAPTAIN HEADED TOWARDS HAGUE, WHEN IT HIT A ROCK, THE TILLER ROPES BURNED AND THE SHIP COULD NOT MANEUVER. THE FIRE RAGED ON AS THE CRAFT SANK AND PASSENGERS JUMPED INTO THE LAKE USING ANYTHING THAT FLOATED AND SWAM TO SHORE. RICHARD SHEAR, THE "RATTLESNAKE MAN," THREW HIS BOX OF SNAKES TO A WOMAN WHO CLIMBED ON IT AND WAS SAVED. THE SHIP'S WRECKAGE STILL LIES NEAR CALAMITY ROCK.

© 2007 MARTY PODSKOCH - SAM GLANZMAN

GREAT SACANDAGA LAKE

EARLY FLOODING IN THE ALBANY AREA

GREAT SACANDAGA LAKE (AKA SACANDAGA RESERVOIR) IN THE SOUTHERN ADIRONDACKS NEAR NORTHVILLE WAS CREATED IN THE LATE 1920s TO CONTROL THE FLOW OF THE SACANDAGA RIVER TO THE HUDSON AND AVOID SPRING FLOODS IN THE ALBANY AREA AND VERY LOW FLOW IN SUMMER, WHICH CLOSED FACTORIES AND CREATED HEALTH HAZARDS. THE VALLEY CONTAINED FARMS, TOWNS, A RAILROAD, AND A RESORT WITH GOLF COURSES, A THEATER, AND AN AMUSEMENT PARK. IN 1927 SOME 12,000 HOMES WERE MOVED OR BURNED AND THOUSANDS WERE MOVED FROM 22 CEMETERIES. THE CONKLINGVILLE DAM WAS COMPLETED IN 1930, 4 MI. WEST OF HADLEY. THE 29-MILE LAKE COVERS 42.3 SQ. MILES. WATER IS RELEASED TO PROVIDE A STEADY FLOW CREATING HYDROELECTRICITY AND YEAR-ROUND RECREATION, INCLUDING BOATING, FISHING, SWIMMING AND SNOWMOBILING. 'SACANDAGA' IS AN INDIAN WORD MEANING 'DROWNED LAND.'

SACANDAGA RESERVOIR

B-47 BOMBER CRASH

A PIECE OF B-47 WRECKAGE

ON JANUARY 16, 1962 AT ABOUT 2 AM, A CREW OF FOUR FLEW A B-47 BOMBER ON A FLIGHT FROM THE PLATTSBURGH AIR FORCE BASE TO PRACTICE LOW-ALTITUDE BOMBING RUNS OVER WATERTOWN NEAR FORT DRUM. WHEN THE PLANE FAILED TO RETURN, A WIDE SCALE SEARCH BEGAN. AFTER MORE THAN FOUR DAYS OF SEARCHING THE SNOW COVERED MOUNTAINS AND LAKES, A PLANE SPOTTED WRECKAGE IN THE HIGH PEAKS REGION. THE B-47 HAD APPARENTLY VEERED ABOUT 30 MILES OFF ITS COURSE IN A STORM AND CLIPPED THE TOP OF WRIGHT'S MOUNTAIN (4,580') STREWING WRECKAGE BETWEEN IT AND ALGONQUIN MT. AFTER A WEEK OF CLIMBING THROUGH SNOW UP TO 20' DEEP SEARCHERS FOUND THREE BODIES, THE 4TH CREWMAN WAS NEVER FOUND. A MEMORIAL TO THESE MEN STANDS NEAR THE CRASH SITE.

© 2005 MARTY POOSKOCH - SAM GLANZMAN

COMMON 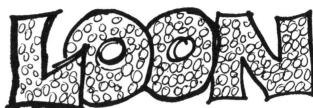 LOON

THE COMMON LOON, ALSO CALLED SPIRIT OF THE NORTH WOODS AND GREAT NORTHERN DIVER, IS FOUND ON MANY LAKES IN THE 'ADIRON- DACKS. ANOTHER NAME, ARISING FROM ITS EERIE CALL ON LONELY LAKES, IS THE SONG OF THE WIL- DERNESS. ITS BODY IS STREAM- LINED WITH DENSE, THICK BONES ENABLING IT TO DIVE DEEPLY FOR FOOD. THE WEBBED FEET, WELL BACK TOWARDS THE TAIL, TURN TO THE SIDE FOR SPEED, BUT IT CANNOT WALK ON LAND.
TO TAKE TO THE AIR IT MUST 'RUN' ON THE WATER, WINGS FLAPPING, FOR A LONG WAY BE- FORE TAKING OFF. LOONS BREED IN THE SPRING AND USUALLY BUILD NESTS NEAR THE SHORE OF ISLANDS. THE FEMALE LAYS 1-2 EGGS. ADULTS MIGRATE IN EARLY NOVEMBER WHILE JUVENILES LEAVE 2 OR 3 WEEKS LATER AND RISK GETTING FROZEN IN. LOONS MIGRATE TO THE OCEAN NEAR LONG ISLAND AND SOMETIMES TO FLOR- IDA. THEY RETURN TO THEIR NATAL LAKE WHEN THE ICE IS GONE. IN 1972 THERE WERE ABOUT 100 PAIRS IN THE ADIRON- DACKS THAT WERE CLASSIFIED AS ENDANGERED, BUT TODAY THERE ARE SOME 250 PAIRS.

© 2006 MARTY PUDSKOCH ~ SAM GLANZMAN

BEAVER RIVER STATION

MAP
BEAVER RIVER
CIRCA 1912

BEAVER RIVER STATION, IN NORTH HERKIMER CO. NEAR THE EASTERN END OF STILLWATER RESERVOIR, IS THE MOST ISOLATED COMMUNITY IN THE ADIRONDACKS. BEGUN IN 1892 WHEN DR. WILLIAM SEWARD WEBB SET UP A STATION ON HIS MOHAWK AND MALONE RR FOR HIS LOGGING OPERATIONS, IT ALSO BECAME A STOP FOR SPORTSMEN. AFTER LOGGING THE AREA, HE KEPT 180 ACRES AND DEEDED THE REST TO THE STATE. IN 1899 WEBB SOLD THE BEAVER RIVER PLOT, WHICH WAS PARCELED FOR CABINS, BOARDING HOUSES, AND HOTELS. WHEN THE RESERVOIR WAS ENLARGED IN 1924, ROADS WERE FLOODED SO SUPPLIES AND PASSENGERS HAD TO COME IN BY RAIL OR BOAT. WHEN ADIRONDACK RAILWAY ENDED SERVICE IN 1964, THE THOMPSON FAMILY, OWNERS OF NORRIDGEWOCK HOTEL AND ITS RESTAURANT, GENERAL STORE, BAR, AND POST OFFICE, BROUGHT IN SUPPLIES BY BOAT OR USED A MODIFIED TRUCK ON THE OLD TRACKS. THERE ARE OVER 100 CAMPS IN BEAVER RIVER STATION BUT ONLY THE THOMPSONS LIVE THERE YEAR ROUND.

©MARTY PODSKOCH – SAM GLANZMAN 2007

A CHRISTMAS STORY

A FOREST RANGER SAW THAT A WHITE SPRUCE HAD BEEN CUT DOWN ON FOREST PRESERVE LAND. FOOTPRINTS IN THE SNOW LED TO A BARN WHERE HE FOUND THE TREE. THE RANGER KNOCKED AT THE HOUSE AND TOLD THE MAN WHO ANSWERED THAT IT WAS A $10 FINE FOR CUTTING THE TREE DOWN. INSIDE CHILDREN WERE PLAYING WITH A LITTER OF PUPPIES. THEIR FATHER, WHO HAD CUT THE TREE DOWN TOOK OUT HIS MONEY, A CRUMPLED $10, A ONE, AND SOME CHANGE. HE HANDED THE $10 TO THE RANGER, WHO COULD SEE THAT MONEY WAS SCARCE HERE, SO HE ASKED IF HE COULD BUY A PUPPY. THE ASTONISHED FATHER TOOK THE $10 BACK AND SMILED IN RELIEF. THE RANGER TOOK THE PUPPY AND LEFT. TWO NIGHTS LATER THE RANGER SAW THE FAMILY IN TOWN AND THE FATHER SAID, "A WHOLE LOT OF FOLK CAME AND BOUGHT OUR PUPPIES, SO WE'RE SHOPPING FOR PRESENTS. OUR CHILDREN, THANKS TO YOU, WILL HAVE A VERY MERRY,

MERRY CHRISTMAS!

ADIRONDACK CHAIRS

IN 1903 THOMAS LEE DESIGNED THE FIRST ADIRONDACK CHAIR, WITH ITS WIDE AND SLOPING SEAT AND BACK, WHILE ON VACATION IN WESTPORT NEAR LAKE CHAMPLAIN. LEE WANTED COMFORTABLE OUTDOOR CHAIRS FOR HIS SUMMER HOME. HE TESTED DIFFERENT DESIGNS ON HIS FAMILY. HE CUT 11 PIECES FROM A SINGLE WIDE BOARD AND MADE A CHAIR WITH A WIDE SEAT, BACK, AND ARMRESTS. LEE LET HIS FRIEND, HARRY BUNNELL, USE HIS DESIGN TO MAKE SOME MONEY THAT WINTER. IN 1905 BUNNELL PATENTED THE "WESTPORT CHAIR" WITHOUT LEE'S PERMISSION. FOR 20 YEARS BUNNELL MADE THESE CHAIRS OUT OF HEMLOCK AND PAINTED THEM DARK BROWN AND GREEN. TODAY THE ADIRONDACK CHAIR IS STILL POPULAR ALL AROUND THE WORLD FOR ITS COMFORT AND ITS MANY DIFFERENT STYLES.

Ⓒ 2005 MARTY PODSKOCH – SAM GLANZMAN

ACKNOWLEDGMENTS

I would first like to thank Sam Glanzman who suggested working together. Without him this project would never have been started. It has been an honor to have him as my illustrator. A special thanks to his wife, Sue who made the weekly trips to the post office to send me Sam's artwork after I moved to Connecticut.

Next I want to thank my wife, Lynn, who has encouraged me and given me the support to continue this project for three years. Also thank you to my children Matthew, Kristy and Ryan for their encouragement and to my son-in-law Matt for his support with computer problems.

Thanks, too, to my parents who provided me with a good education that would enable me to go on this adventure in writing.

A warm thank you to all those who encouraged me and provided valuable assistance in bringing this book into print, especially:

My dedicated editor, David Hayden, was always there to correct and guide me. I never would have completed this project without his insightful questions and suggestions.

Publisher Wray Rominger, who gave me the opportunity to write my first book and provided advice for this book.

Cris Meixner of the *Hamilton County Times*, the first Adirondack newspaper to publish my stories; Mark Frost of *The Chronicle* in Glens Falls; Adam Atkinson, *of The Journal Republican in* Lowville, Tom Henecker and Katy Odell of *The North Creek News-Enterprise*; John Gereau of Denton Publishing in Elizabethtown; Joe Kelly, editor and publisher of *The Boonville Herald, and Bert More, editor* of the *Delaware County Times,* who published my stories in my old hometown of Delhi, NY.

I am grateful for the research material and photographs gathered for me by these libraries and librarians: Jerry Pepper, Adirondack Museum Library; Bruce Cole, Crandall Public Library; Michelle Tucker, Saranac Lake Library; Neil Suprenant, Paul Smith's College Library; Patty Prindle and Dick Tucker, Society for the Protection of the Adirondacks Library, Niskayuna; Donna Ripp, Erwin Library, Boonville; Karen Glass, Keene Valley Library; Isabella Worthen and Karen Lee, Old Forge Library; Susan Doolittle and Margaret Gibbs, Essex County Historical Society Library, Elizabethtown; Jackie Viestenz, Sherman Library, Port Henry; David Minnich, Wead Library, Malone; and Cathy Johnson, Lynn Oles, and Florence Grill, The Cannon Free Library, Delhi.

Thank you to these people for sharing their photos and information: Liz Defazio, Lake Placid Olympic Museum; Laura Foster, Frederic Remington Art Museum; Fred Provancha, Ticonderoga Heritage Museum; and Brother Arnold, Sabbathday Lake Shaker Village, New Gloucester, Maine.

To these historians and societies, thank you for opening your files and sharing your pictures: Peg Masters, Town of Webb; MaryEllen Salls, Town of Brighton; Bill Frenette, Tupper Lake; Marvin Bissell, Town of Newcomb; Bill Zullow, Indian Lake; Bill Gates, Bolton Landing; Ermina Pincombe, Hamilton County Historical Society; Joan Daby, Iron Museum, Port Henry; Betty Osolin, Schroon Lake-North

Hudson Historical Society; Sue Perkins & Caryl A. Hopson, Herkimer County Historical Society; John Simons, Piseco Historical Society; Carol Poole, Franklin County Historical Society; and Gail Murray, Town of Webb Historical Society, Old Forge.

A special thanks to these individuals and writers who gave information and helped proofread captions: Marilyn Cross, Ticonderoga; George Cataldo, Glenfield; Don Williams, Gloversville; Jack Freeman, Adirondack Mountain Club, Lake George; Terry Perkins, Stillwater; Adam Atkinson, Lowville; Janet Chapman, Tupper Lake; Libby Cassella, Barton Mines; Virginia Brandreth, Brandreth Park; Nate Pedrick, Adirondack Bats, Dolgeville; Steven Engelhart, Adirondack Architectural Heritage, Keesville; Gary Lee, Inlet; Dot Liberty, North Hudson; Jay O'Hern, Camden; Doug Wolfe, Wilmington; and Jim Shea Sr., Lake Placid.

43 O'Neill Lane,
East Hampton, Connecticut 06424
860.267.2442
podskoch@comcast.net
http://www.cccstories.com

Podskoch family at home on Lake Pocotopaug: 1st row l-r, Jenna & Vinnie Podskoch, Lydia & Kira Roloff, Lynn & Marty. Second row: Ryan Podskoch, Kristy & Matt Roloff, and back row Matt Podskoch

BIBLIOGRAPHY ADIRONDACK STORIES

Aber, Ted and King, Stella. *The History of Hamilton County*, Lake Pleasant, NY: Great Wilderness Books, 1965.

Aber, Ted. *Adirondack Folks*, Prospect, NY: Prospect Books, 1980.

Bensen, *Arthur L. The Story of a New York City Tenderfoot and His Adirondack Mountain Adventure*, North Hudson , NY: Frontier Town Productions Inc., n.d.

Bird, Norton Bus, *Changing Times in the Adirondacks: Portraying the Extraordinary Life of a True Adirondack Native*, n.p., n.d.

Bogdan, Robert. *Adirondack Vernacular, The Photography of Henry M. Beach*, Syracuse: Syracuse University Press, 2003.

Bridger, Beverly. *Mrs. Vanderbilt's Sagamore*, Raquette Lake, NY: Sagamore Institute of the Adirondacks, n. d.

Brown, William H. Editor *History of Warren County New York*, Glens Falls: Board of Supervisors of Warren County/ Glens Falls Post Company, 1963.

Carson, Russell M. L. *Peaks and People of the Adirondacks*, Garden City: Doubleday, Duran & Co., 1928.

Cohen, Linda; Cohen, Sarah and Peg Masters, *Old Forge, Gateway to the Adirondacks*, Charleston, SC: Arcadia Publishing, 2003.

Collins, Geraldine. *The Biography and Funny Sayings of Paul Smith*, Paul Smiths, NY: Paul Smith's College, 1965.

Colvin, Verplanck. *Seventh Annual Report on the progress of the Topographical Survey of the Adirondack Region of New York*. Albany, NY: Weed, Parsons and Co., 1880.

Conservation Department of the State of New York.

Annual Reports, 1927-65.

Cross, David & Potter, Joan. *Adirondack Firsts*, Elizabethtown, NY: Pinto Press, 1992.

DeSormo, Maitland C. *Heydays of the Adirondacks*. Saranac Lake, NY: North Country Books, 1975.

_____. *Summers on the Saranacs*, Saranac Lake, NY: Adirondacks Yesterdays Inc., 1980.

Donaldson, Alfred L. *A History of the Adirondacks*, 2 vols., New York: Century Company, 1921.

Engle, Robert; Kirschenbaum, Howard; Malo, Paul. *Santanoni From Japanese Temple to Life at an Adirondack Great Camp*, Keesville, NY: Adirondack Architectural Heritage, 2000.

Fennessy, Lana. *The History of Newcomb*, Newcomb, NY: Lana Fennessey, 1996.

Fowler, Albert editor *Cranberry Lake from Wilderness to Adirondack Park*, Syracuse, NY: The Adirondack Museum/Syracuse University Press, 1968.

Fowler, Barney. *Adirondack Album*, Schenectady, NY: Outdoor Associates, 1974.

_____. *Adirondack Album Volume Two*, Schenectady, NY: Outdoor Associates, 1980.

_____. *Adirondack Album Volume Three*, Schenectady, NY: Outdoor Associates, 1982.

Gallos, Phil. *By Foot in the Adirondacks*, Saranac Lake, NY: Adirondack Publishing Company, Inc., 1972.

Gates, Thomas A. *Adirondack Lakes*. Charleston, SC: Arcadia Publishing, 2004.

Gates, William Preston. *Lake George Boats and Steamboats*, Queensbury, NY: W. P. Gates Publishing Co., 2003.

Gilborn, Craig. *Durant The Fortunes and Woodland Camps of a Family in the Adirondacks*, Blue Mountain Lake, NY: The Adirondack Museum, 1981.

Grady, Joseph F. *The Adirondacks Fulton Chain-Big Moose region The Story of a Wilderness*, Boonville, NY: The Willard Press, 1933.

Graham, Frank Jr. *The Adirondack Park, A Political History*, New York: Alfred A. Knopf, 1978.

Healy, Bill. *The High Peaks of Essex The Adirondack Mountains of Orson Schofield Phelps*, Fleischmanns, NY: Purple Mountain Press, 1992.

Hochschild, Harold. *Adirondack Steamboats on Raquette Lake and Blue Mountain Lakes*, Blue Mountain Lake, NY: Adirondack Museum of the Adirondack Historical Association, 1974.

_____. *Doctor Durant and his Iron Horse*, Blue Mountain Lake: Adirondack Museum of the Adirondack Historical Association, 1971.

_____. *Lumberjacks and Rivermen in the Central Adirondacks 1850-1950*, Blue Mountain Lake, NY: Adirondack Museum of the Adirondack Historical Association, 1974.

_____. *The Macintyre Mine-from Failure to Fortune*, Blue Mountain Lake: Adirondack Museum of the Adirondack Historical Association, 1976.

Historical Book Committee. *Sesquicentennial of the Town of Arietta Hamilton County New York* Arietta, NY: Historical Book Committee Town of Arietta, 1986.

Horrell, Jeffrey L. *Seneca Ray Stoddard Transforming the Adirondack Wilderness in Text and Image*, Syracuse, NY: Syracuse University Press, 1999.

Hyde, Floy S. *Adirondack Forests, Fields and Mines.* Lakemont, NY: North Country Books, 1974.

_____. *Water over the Dam at Mountain View in the Adirondacks, Early Resort Days in the Great North Woods*, New York: Vail Ballou Press Inc., 1970.

Jaques, Adeline F. *Echoes from Whiteface Mountain, A Brief History of Willmington, New York.* Wilmington, NY: n. p., 1980.

Jennings, Virginia. *The Day the Town Died*, n. p., n.d.,

Kaiser, Harvey H. *Great Camps of the Adirondacks*, Boston: David R. Goodine Publisher, Inc., 1982.

Kanze, Edward. *The World of John Burroughs, The Life and Work of one of America's Greatest Naturalist*, San Francisco: Sierra Club Books, 1996.

Keith, Herbert F. *Man of the Woods*, Syracuse, NY: Syracuse University Press/The Adirondack Museum, 1972.

Keller, Jane Eblen. *Adirondack Wilderness, A Story of Man and Nature*, Syracuse, NY: Syracuse University Press, 1980.

Kudish, Michael. *Where did the tracks go?* Saranac Lake, NY: Chauncy Press, 1985.

Lynn, Peggy. And Weber, *Sandra. Breaking Trail, Remarkable Women of the Adirondacks*, Fleischmanns, NY: Purple Mountain Press, 2004.

McMartin, Barbara. *The Great Forests of the Adirondacks.* Utica, NY: North Country Books, 1998.

_____. *Hides, Hemlocks and Adirondack History: How the Tanning Industry Influenced the Region's Growth*, Utica, NY: North Country Books, 1992.

_____. *Discover the Eastern Adirondacks*, Canada Lake, NY: Lake View Press, 1998.

Monaghan, Jay. *The Great Rascal The Life and Adventures of Ned Buntline*, New York: Bonanza Books, 1951.

O'Hern, William J. *Adirondack Characters and Campfire Yarns, Early Settlers and Their Traditions.* Cleveland, NY: The Forager Press, 2005.

O'Kane, Walter Collins. *Trails and Summits of the Adirondacks*, Boston: Houghton Mifflin Company, 1928.

Pilcher, Edith. *A Centennial History of the Association for the Protection of the Adirondacks: 1901 –2003.* Niskayuna, NY: Association for the Protection of the Adirondacks, 2003.

Sattler, Jennifer Gordon. *All Aboard, Owney! The Adirondack Mail Dog*, Utica: Nicholas K. Burns Publishing, 2003.

Schneider, Paul. *The Adirondacks: A History of America's First Wilderness*, New York: Henry Holt and Company, 1998.

Seaver, Frederick J. *Historical Sketches of Franklin County and Its Several Towns*, Albany, NY: J. B. Lyon Co., 1918.

Simmons, Louis J. *Mostly Spruce and Hemlock*. Tupper Lake: Vail-Ballou Press Inc., 1976.

Sleicher, Charles Albert. *The Adirondacks: American Playground*. New York: Exposition Press, 1960.

Smeby, Susan Thomas. *Cranberry Lake and Wanakena*, Charleston SC: Arcadia Publishing, 2003.

Steinberg, Michael. *Our Wilderness*, Lake George: Adirondack Mountain Club. Inc., 1992.

Stoddard, Seneca Ray. Edited by Maitland C. De Sormo. *Old times in the Adirondacks, The Narrative of a trip into the Wilderness in 1873*, Burlington, VT: George Little Press, 1971.

Trimm, Ruth. *Raquette Lake, A Time to Remember*, Utica, NY: North Country Books Inc., 1989.

Webb, Nina H. *Footsteps Through the Adirondacks*, Utica, NY: North Country Books, 1996.

Weber, Sandra. *Two in the Wilderness*, Honesdale, PA: Boyds Mills Press, 2005.

White, William Chapman. *Adirondack Country*, New York: Duell, Sloan & Pierce, 1954.

Williams, Donald. *Inside the Adirondack Blue Line*, Utica: North Country Books, 1999.

_____. *The Adirondacks 1931-1990*, Charleston SC: Arcadia Publishing, 2003.

_____. *Along the Adirondack Trail*, Charleston SC: Arcadia Publishing, 2004.

_____. *The Saga of Nicholas Stoner A Tale of the Adirondacks*, Utica, NY: North Country Books, 1972.

Pamphlets

Franklin Historical Review ,Vol. 15 1978 "Bootlegging-A Way of Life" Smallman, C. Walter 27-45. Franklin County Historical and Museum Society, Malone, NY

Franklin Historical Review Vol. 4 1967 " Black Horse Troop, Elizabeth Donovan

Magazine

The Shaker Quarterly Volume VII, No. 3 Fall 1967 pp. 99-106.

Newspapers

Adirondack Daily Enterprise, Saranac Lake, NY

Adirondack Enterprise, Elizabethtown, NY

Elizabethtown Post, Elizabethtown, NY

Lake Placid News, Lake Placid, NY

Lowville Journal and Republican, Lowville, NY

Malone Farmer, Malone, NY

Saint Regis Falls Adirondack News, St. Regis Falls, NY

Ticonderoga Sentinel, Ticonderoga, NY

The Tupper Lake Free Press, Tupper Lake, NY

ABOUT THE AUTHOR AND ILLUSTRATOR

Marty Podskoch, a retired reading teacher, is the author of three other books: *Fire Towers of the Catskills: Their History and Lore* (2000); *Adirondack Fire Towers: Their History and Lore, the Southern Districts* (2003); *Adirondack Fire Towers: Their History and Lore, the Northern Districts* (2005).

While gathering stories of the forest rangers and fire tower observers, he became fascinated with other aspects of the Adirondacks such as the logging and mining industries, the individualistic men who guided sportsmen, the hotels they stayed in, the animals, railroads, etc.

When Sam Glanzman, a noted comic book illustrator, asked to work on a project with Marty in 2003, Marty suggested writing a weekly newspaper column, "Adirondack Stories," that he would write and Sam would illustrate. Many newspapers in and around the Adirondacks began publishing the column.

After three years they decided to publish this book with 150 illustrated panels from their newspaper column. They are now continuing this successful series.

Marty and his wife, Lynn, live in Colchester, CT where they are close to their family and two granddaughters, Kira and Lydia. He enjoys hiking in the nearby Salmon River Forest and is doing research on the CCC camps of the Adirondacks and Connecticut.

Sam Glanzman is a comic book legend. Over a period of 60 years he has illustrated thousands of pages of comic book art. Here are a few comic books that he has illustrated: Hercules, War at Sea, Army Heroes, Sgt. Rock, Kona, Attu, Spitfire Comics, Zorro, Turock, The Loser's Special, Space Adventures, DC Special Blue Ribbon Digest, Our Army at War, Air War Stories, A Sailor's Story, Semper Fi, The Best of DC, House of Secrets, Jungle Tales of Tarzan, and Flying Saucers.

He was born in Baltimore, Maryland in 1924. Sam began working for publishers such as Centaur and Harvey. He then served aboard a destroyer, the USS Stevens, in the South Pacific during WW II. On board he kept a diary that served as a foundation for his future work. He is considered by many to be the ultimate war artist.

Once out of the Navy he began illustrating children's books for Random House and Grosset & Dunlop.

During the early 1950s, Sam began illustrating for Classic Comic books. From there he picked up other publishing accounts: Charlton, Dell, DC Comics, Marvel, and others.

Then in the 1960s and 70s Sam illustrated the long-running Outdoor Life feature, "This Happened to Me."

"I am not a cartoonist but rather a free lance illustrator," said Sam. "My art for the comic books is of an illustrative style not cartoons."

Sam and his wife, Sue, live in Maryland, NY.

About the Author

Marty Podskoch with his granddaughters, Lydia and Kira Roloff.
Courtesy of A. Beauchemin

Marty Podskoch was a reading teacher for 28 years at Delaware Academy in Delhi, NY. He retired in 2001. Marty and his wife, Lynn, raised their three children, Matt, Kristy, and Ryan, in a renovated 19th c. farmhouse along the West Branch of the Delaware River. He became interested in fire towers after climbing to the fire tower on Hunter Mountain in the fall of 1987. He met the observer, who was in his 60s, chatted with him, and listened to his stories. Marty was hooked. He set out on a quest to find out all he could about the history and lore of the fire towers.

In 1997 Wray Rominger of Purple Mountain Press asked Marty to write about the history of the Catskill fire towers and the restoration project that was occurring in the Catskills.

After interviewing over 100 observers, rangers, and their families, Marty had gathered hundreds of stories and pictures about the 23 fire towers in the Catskill region. In 2000, *Fire Towers of the Catskills: Their History and Lore* was published by Purple Mountain Press, which also published his second book, *Adirondack Fire Towers: Their History and Lore, the Southern Districts*, in June of 2003 and his third title, *Adirondack Fire Towers: Their History and Lore, the Northern Districts*, in November of 2005.

Marty also wrote a weekly newspaper column, "Adirondack Stories" in five area newspapers. Sam Glanzman, a noted comic book illustrator for the past 50 years, illustrated the stories. After five years of weekly columns Podskoch Press published 251 illustrated stories in two volumes, *Adirondack Stories:*

Historical Sketches and *Adirondack Stories II: 101 More Historical Sketches.*

In 2011 Podskoch wrote and published *Adirondack Civilian Conservation Corps Camps: History, Memories & Legacy of the CCC.*

In the Fall of 2013 Podskoch received the "Arthur E. Newkirk Education Award" from the Adirondack Mountain Club for his work in preserving the history of the fire towers and Civilian Conservation Corps Camps in the Adirondacks and Catskills.

The Adirondack 102 Club: Your Passport and Guide to the North Country was published in 2014. It is a comprehensive guide to travelers listing the history and interesting places to visit in all 102 towns and villages in the Adirondacks. It is also a journal and passport, a place to get each town stamped or signed by a store or resident. Your chance to discover the secret and lovely places that the main roads do not reveal. Those that achieve this goal receive a Vagabond patch.

After eight years of research, his book *Connecticut Civilian Conservation Corps Camps: History, Memories & Legacy of the CCC* was published in 2016.

Presently he is writing books on the CCC Camps of Rhode Island, The Connecticut 169 Club, and The History of East Hampton/Chatham.

For further information contact:
Marty Podskoch
43 O'Neill Lane
East Hampton, CT 06424
860.267.2442